Longman Exam Practice Kits

A-level British and European Modern History

Edward Townley

LONGMAN

Series editors
Geoff Black and Stuart Wall

Titles available

A-level

Biology	Geography
British and European Modern History	German
Business Studies	Mathematics
Chemistry	Physics
Economics	Psychology
French	Sociology

Addison Wesley Longman Ltd,
Edinburgh Gate, Harlow,
CM20 2JE, England
and Associated Companies throughout the World

First published 1997

ISBN 0582 312452

British Library Cataloguing-in-Publication Data
A catalogue record for this book is available from the British Library.

Set by 35 in 11/13pt Baskerville

Produced by Longman Singapore Publishers Pte
Printed in Singapore

Acknowledgements

In writing this *Exam Practice Kit* I have received considerable help from many
members of the staff of Addison Wesley Longman and of the Guidelines
Partnership. I thank them all. My other principal debt is to my fellow A-level
history examiners on whose expertise and friendship I have relied for so many
years.

Edward Townley

Contents

How to use this book

This book covers the major topics in A-level British and European Modern History. The book is split into four parts.

Part I Preparing for the examination

This section covers what you should be doing before and during the examination. The different types of questions that you will face in the examination are considered, together with the techniques that you will need to show in order to answer each type of question successfully.

Part II Topic outlines, revision activities and practice questions

In each topic chapter you will find the following:

1 **Revision tips**   These tips give some useful revision hints that should help you to learn the key facts of the topic more easily. Try to revise the same subject in different ways: drawing up lists, charts and analysing problems as part of revision.

2 **Topic outline**   This section briefly summarizes the key points and historical arguments related to that particular topic area. Helpful suggestions about the sort of angle that examination questions are likely to take are also provided: use these to help you to focus your revision. The notes in the topic outline will not replace your own full notes but may give you new ideas and ways of approaching that topic area. Make sure that you can expand more fully on the key facts identified in the topic area. At the end of each topic outline some useful information (including important terms, figures, statistics and key dates) is also given.

3 **Revision activities**   These exercises are aimed at making your revision active. They will help you to self-check your understanding of that topic area.

4 **Practice questions**   These questions are very similar to the type of question you are likely to face in the examination; and include essay questions and document questions. Remember that the more practice you get at answering questions the better. You need to learn how to analyse and interpret a question, applying the facts and knowledge you have assimilated. Practice at writing both essay plans and full essays under timed conditions is useful. Try hard to answer the questions fully before you look at the suggested answers in *Part III*.

Part III Answers and grading

Here you will find suggested answers to revision activities and practice questions. Answers are not provided for *all* the revision activities; you should check your answers against your class notes or textbooks. The answers provided should give you further ideas on how to approach the question with the aim of improving and developing your own answers.

Part IV Timed practice paper

It is difficult to provide a specimen history examination paper which will meet the majority of circumstances. The paper provided is, therefore, a combination of document and essay questions. You should allow yourself the time that is stated at the start of the paper. Full answers are supplied for the document questions, and outline answers are given for the essay questions.

part I
Preparing for the examination

Preparing for the examination

REVISING FOR A- AND AS-LEVEL HISTORY – INTRODUCTION

If you have been studying history effectively during your course then revision will come as a natural continuation of your normal study. If you are not sure whether you have been an effective history student then, if time permits, it could pay you to obtain one of the history study guides that are on the market. The *Longman Study Guide on Modern History* for example, will give you systematic information on study techniques. If you are already within days of the examination then forget this advice and rely on what follows in the various sections of this book.

Important features of good study and good revision technique

► Check through what past examination papers and the syllabus tell you about the topics which are likely to be on your paper.
► Read and revise by thinking about historical problems; do not just learn facts.
► Do as much reading as the rest of your commitments allow but read around issues (problems again), preferably in short sessions. Try to read quickly by actively searching for ideas to help with a problem or historical information to support a point you want to make.
► Keep your revision note summaries brief and make sure that they relate to possible examination questions, even if indirectly.
► Practise writing history, especially under timed conditions, and take a pride in writing as well as you can.
► Master the vocabulary of the examination paper and also the specialist vocabulary used by historians.

Planning revision

Drawing up a revision plan should be a stimulus to a lot of useful activity but first read through all of Part I of this book:

► Use the revision planner and the topic areas in this book to give you a personal revision framework.
► Carry out a survey of what needs to be done but be realistic rather than ambitious.
► Count up the likely number of work days before the examination and then count up the number of tasks you feel you should attempt in order to do well in each paper.
► Do some simple arithmetic to see how long is available for each revision task in the light of all your other commitments.
► Prune the list as necessary and also set yourself revision priorities, decide what simply must be done and what may have to be regarded as a bonus.
► Plan to do your history revision in short bursts, separated by other work or play.
► Get started.

How to revise

In the revision period it is important that you follow a study pattern that works for you. If the advice which follows does not fit in with your normal work pattern then you will almost certainly do better by sticking to the techniques with which you have become familiar:

▶ Look through the list of topics on which you have made notes during your course and put down the headings in a list.

▶ Examine the recent past papers on the options you are taking.

▶ Draw up a list, in order of priority, of the topics it seems wise to study. This list should be based first on the pattern and frequency of questions on past papers and then reflect your own interests within the syllabus content.

▶ If there are compulsory sections or questions in any of your papers then make sure your selection of topics takes this into account.

▶ Draw a revision diagram and place arrows on it to show any links between subject matter so that you can get double value for some of your revision and also prepare yourself for questions that stray across the usual topic boundaries.

▶ Set yourself targets for revision and keep a chart plotting your progress. You need to know if you are falling behind in what you had planned to do so that your schedule can be changed. There is little point in revising half a syllabus thoroughly but never getting round to tackling the other half.

▶ Make sure that you have time away from revision to enjoy yourself and to get some exercise.

Using examination papers in revision

Making yourself familiar with the questions you will have to face and practising answering them directly are central to good examination revision. Do not simply revise your notes and learn lots of historical information. A moment's thought should tell you how little of your knowledge you will have time to put on paper within the strict time limits of the examination. History is not just concerned with describing what happened in the past but with interpreting how and why things happened as they did. It is about solving problems relating to the past. Study of past examination papers will show what problems interest the examiners who have set your paper and will give you the most direct route to acquiring the skills you will need to solve these problems. The topic outlines later in this book give lots of examples of how to go about this.

HISTORY EXAMINATION PAPERS

There are variations between the examination boards and so it is very important that, in your study and revision, you use the papers of the board for which you are entered. The main points to note when revising are:

▶ How many questions you have to answer.

▶ Any examination regulations concerning answering questions from different sections of the paper or answering compulsory questions. These must always be observed, for the likely penalty is that 'illegal' answers will be ignored by the examiners.

▶ The difference in terms of questions between option papers covering a short period of time or a strictly defined topic and the so-called outline papers often spread across the centuries.

▶ Option papers almost always include one or two compulsory questions on historical documents and these will normally make up half of the marks for that paper.

▶ Examination boards are taking steps to remove the 'lottery' in question choice on outline papers, some of which have forty or more questions available. They are guaranteeing questions on certain broadly defined topics within the syllabus. This can be a great help in terms of organizing revision but note that the topics are broad and the questions on some of them may not be to your liking. You need to cover a range of such guaranteed topics in order to have some element of examination choice. To find out whether your examination board guarantees topics and what these are you will need to gain access to the board's examination syllabus. Copies of this are usually provided free to all examination centres but not to individual candidates. If guaranteed topics have only just been introduced, then past papers will not help in seeing what questions are being asked under the new arrangements and you will have to rely totally on the syllabus.

Document questions

These commonly occupy half of one of the two A-level examination papers and, although questions differ between boards, a pattern of sub-questions usually runs from year to year. It is almost invariably sensible to answer the document questions before any essay questions. Considerable concentration is required to read through the extracts at speed and each of the sub-questions requires a new start: the complexity of all this is best faced when fresh at the beginning of the examination.

Patterns of sub-questions

You need to familiarize yourself with the pattern of sub-questions used by your examination board; a common one for 25 marks is:

(a) simply identifying a term or people referred to in the documents   *(2 marks)*
(b) explaining the argument in one of the documents   *(4 marks)*
(c) comparing the evidence in one document with that in another or discussing how far the two documents agree with each other on some issue   *(4 marks)*
(d) describing in what ways the language (and the tone) of one document promote the author's purpose   *(4 marks)*
(e) noting the origins of one (or more) document(s) and explaining why a historian might consider it to be of value and yet wish to treat it with caution   *(4 marks)*
(f) using the evidence in these documents and your own knowledge to explain why . . .   *(7 marks)*

An alternative (f) might read 'From your own knowledge examine how full an account of (the topic) can be constructed from **the evidence in** these documents', which involves explaining what of value is in the documents for this purpose and then, from your own knowledge, indicating what is not there or there only in an unsatisfactory form. Note here the words which I have put in bold print and which make it clear that it is the content of the document and not its origins with which you are concerned.

In answering document questions:

▶ Relate the amount you write to the mark tariff on offer . . . a word or two for 1 mark, a paragraph for 4 marks and a page for 7 marks is a simple rule, but be a bit flexible.

▶ Read the documents quickly before you start so that you have the overall feel of what their range is and what the issues are.

▶ Try to cite evidence in the documents which supports your analysis but do this briefly; it is *not* usually enough just to refer to the numbers of the lines in the documents.

▶ Despite all the complexity try not to exceed the time allowed for the question. If there are two document and two essay questions in three hours and each is worth 25 marks then the time available is 45 minutes. Try (very hard indeed) in these circumstances not to go beyond 50 minutes, at the most, for each of the document questions.

Despite this advice you are unlikely to do well unless you have had extensive document question practice, some of it under timed conditions, prior to the examination. If, during your course, this practice has been neglected then some of your revision time should be spent on it. The examination is not competitive so this could be an ideal opportunity to do some group revision to everyone's benefit.

Essay questions

The standard challenge set by the examiners is for the candidate to complete four essay answers in three hours and this usually accounts for half the marks in the A-level history examination:

▶ each question is usually marked out of 25.
▶ grade boundaries can vary marginally from year to year depending for example on the examiners' assessment of the difficulty of the paper in the light of the answers from candidates.

Essay marks

▶ The normal pass (bottom E grade) mark for an essay will be 10.
▶ Four marks each worth 15 will give a B grade.
▶ The most interesting marks for an essay under this scheme of marking are 15 and 16.
▶ A mark of 15 will have lots of historical information and, equally important, a number of comments which relate to the terms of the question set. The answer may well tell the story of what happened but the comments raise this into a relevant answer to the problem or issue posed in the question.
▶ Marks down from 15 will have fewer comments until, at around 11 and 12 marks, they simply give an account of what happened with the terms of the question forgotten.
▶ Below 11 the account will have errors, gaps and irrelevant passages and, with enough of these weaknesses, will fail to reach A-level standard.
▶ The mark of 16 indicates that the candidate has risen above just telling the story and commenting but has seen that there is an issue involved in the question and has tried to provide a directly argued or analytical answer. Such an answer rises above the historical information the candidate has available and the factual knowledge becomes the servant of the answer. The chronological historical narrative is abandoned and historical information is organized in support of an argument or analysis.
▶ The higher marks above 16 will go to analytical or argued answers which are particularly well constructed, particularly well supported by sound knowledge or contain especially perceptive insights. These answers have, however, got to this position only because they are, above all, direct answers set in the terms of the question.
▶ Candidates wanting an A grade will need to be able to produce the 16 or 16+ answer. How to do this cannot be learned just in the pre-examination revision time, though an awareness of what is needed at this high level may greatly improve the able candidate's chances of an A grade.
▶ For other candidates there is a simpler message that, in the narrative essays which most of us write, explaining what happened, the more and better comments you can make which tie the narrative into the question, the better your prospects of getting a B or C grade.

Other essay tips

▶ Pause before you start to write and think how you are going to answer the question. This is the last moment at which you can decide to answer the question directly (by analysis and argument) rather than just tell the story of what happened.

► Make an essay plan but keep it very brief, probably just a series of key words which make sense to you in terms of the comments you want to make or the areas of the topic you must not forget to mention. There is little point in producing a plan based just on factual content nor for using sentences and other elaborations in your plan. Rather get on with the essay.

► Avoid rambling or long introductions. If you know the theme that you are going to argue it is probably easiest to give this as your introduction.

► Try to structure your essay round paragraphs. It may be too simple to suggest a paragraph per idea but paragraphs can help you to think in terms of arguing and commenting relevantly. Without paragraphs the temptation is just to go on describing what happened and forget the need to answer the problem set.

► Pause occasionally (and briefly!) to ask whether you are still answering the question.

► Avoid slang and casual English. You will not lose marks directly but it undermines the effectiveness of your argument. Long before the examination make sure you have built up a good historical and general vocabulary.

► Make sure that you leave enough time to write a worthwhile answer to the last question on the paper. It is far easier to earn the first few marks out of 25 than it is, by writing more on an earlier answer, to raise a mark from say 13 to 15. The most certain way to fail the examination is by not even starting the last question.

► If you have not organized your time well, then at least get down an outline answer to the last question rather than write nothing. It is better for any such notes to be based on the ideas (comments) you would have made rather than giving a list of factual content.

► Always attempt a concluding paragraph but avoid just repeating your essay. One good conclusion is to give an order of priority to the points you have made or say which seems to you to be the most important of them.

COMMAND WORDS IN HISTORY QUESTIONS

In history papers these are sometimes not as useful as in other subjects, for examiners sometimes seem to use words as much to give variety to the appearance of the questions on the paper as to indicate some precise approach to the question that the candidate should have in mind. However, some guidance is possible and the following terms appear regularly:

► '**To what extent** was the collapse of the Tsarist government in Russia brought about by the personal incompetence of Nicholas II?' and, closely related, '**How far do you agree that** Disraeli was more important as an imperialist than as a social reformer?' These questions are often most easily answered by first discussing in what ways the statement is valid (true) and then going on to suggest what other points also need to be made to explain or modify the claim in the question.

► '**Examine** the causes of the Spanish Civil War.' This lends itself to making a brief list of the causes, so that none is omitted, and then a brief discussion of each one with a conclusion linking them together or suggesting which were the most important.

► '**Discuss** the opinion that the First World War was caused by a series of accidents' or used with a quotation as in ' "More important for the abuses it left untouched than for those it remedied:" discuss this opinion of the 1832 Parliamentary Reform Act.' This type of question offers a controversial or sweeping statement, usually for you to challenge. Discuss the value of the proposition and then feel free to say that it is only part of the story. You can then go on to say what else needs to be considered or how you disagree with the claim. Do not just assert that the proposition is nonsense and immediately go on to propose other factors, for examiners may then suspect you are dodging the question.

▶ **'How valid . . .'** is an important term in document questions when it asks how valid a piece of evidence is. You will then need to imagine yourself as a historian of the topic and think how far you would trust the document. You would consider both its origins and its content to form an impression of this. 'How valid . . .' in essay questions is much less technical and usually simply means how far do you agree, for example, 'How valid is it to argue that the Boer War marked a turning-point in British foreign policy?'

DURING THE EXAMINATION

A few pieces of practical advice:

▶ Look through the paper quickly and identify possible questions, select the one you will do first and also note your likely second choice, for this will give you confidence. You can still change your mind.

▶ Do not delude yourself. The results of the 1832 Parliamentary Reform Act are not the same topic as the causes of the Reform Act and you will get little, if any, credit for writing an answer to a question you have invented for yourself. Better to look elsewhere in the paper.

▶ Pause for a moment before you even start to plan. Think what is the most direct attack on the problem which the question presents. If you plunge in you might do no more than tell the story.

▶ Take the same approach with all the later questions.

▶ Keep an eye on the time and allocate it sensibly between questions, by all means take a little longer over a favourite question but only a very few minutes more. Your quick opening survey of questions should have given a clue as to how many good questions there are.

▶ But, however thin your choices are, make a determined attempt to open up your last answer rather than go on polishing earlier efforts.

▶ If you write too much you are, again, probably just telling the story rather than answering the question as it is set.

If you have time, read through your answers but do not bank on this. Add extra points even if you have to scribble them in the margin but do not make your script unreadable or start crossing passages out at this stage. Anything crossed out will be ignored by the examiners. They are unlikely to knock marks off for things that are there, so leave well alone.

HISTORY COURSEWORK

This does not really come into the revision period, for submission dates are usually earlier in the year. With this task out of the way you will have more time for revision and fewer, or shorter, examination papers to take. Take full advantage of this to prepare yourself thoroughly.

HOW TO USE THE FOLLOWING SECTIONS OF THIS EXAMINATION KIT

Work systematically through those of the eight topic outlines in Part II on which you hope to answer questions. At the end of each topic outline, revision activities and practice questions are given. You should try to work at least some of these out before turning to the answers suggested in Part III. In Part II each topic outline also includes other revision ideas and you should treat these as examples of the revision techniques you can apply to any of your revision topics. Part IV provides an example of a timed history examination paper. You can use this for general information or, more usefully, to attempt to answer appropriate questions under timed examination conditions before looking at the suggested answers and trying to improve them.

part II

Topic outlines, revision activities and practice questions

British domestic history 1815–68

✓ **REVISION TIPS**

Draw up a list of appropriate political revision topics in chronological order, for example:

▶ Tory governments 1815–22 and 1822–30
  – 1815–22 Lord Liverpool and the issue of public disorder and government repression
  – 1822–27 Lord Liverpool and the Liberal (Enlightened) Tories
  – 1827–30 Disintegration of the Tories
▶ Whig reforms 1830–41
  – 1830–32 The Whigs and the passing of the 1832 Parliamentary Reform Act
  – 1833–41 Whig governments and their later reforms
▶ 1829–46 Career of Peel including 1838–46 repeal of the Corn Laws
▶ 1838–48 Chartism
▶ 1846–68 Parliamentary instability

Realize that the politics of the period 1846–68 was very complicated and that it is difficult to find clear-cut revision topics there but at least look up what Disraeli and Gladstone did in those years (ready for a question on either man going beyond 1868). If you have revised the 1832 Parliamentary Reform Act then revise also the 1867 Act. The conditions which, in the 1850s and 1860s, favoured the emergence of the Liberal Party, both in parliament and in the country at large, form another useful revision topic, linking political history with social history.

Draw up a list of appropriate social and economic revision topics (check first that such questions have appeared in past papers), for example:

▶ poverty and the Poor Law (especially the 1834 Poor Law Amendment Act)
▶ public health legislation (especially the 1848 Public Health Act) and living conditions
▶ educational provision
▶ factory conditions and legislation
▶ the creation of a railway network after 1830 together with its economic and social effects
▶ religion, its role in society and as a source of humanitarian reforms

Do not just revise in terms of factual recall. Revise through problem-solving, for example:

▶ Was there a great change (a watershed) in the nature of the Tory governments in the year 1822? Form an opinion of their nature pre-1822 then post-1822 (to the death of Lord Liverpool in 1827). What information can you use to support the idea of a watershed and what points to a different conclusion? (Consult the Topic Outline below.)
▶ To what extent did the Whig reforms 1833–41 solve the social problems of the day?
▶ Did Peel create a new Tory (Conservative) Party in the 1830s and destroy it in 1846?
▶ To what extent did the 1834 Poor Law solve the problem of the poor in society?

In each case:

► Collect information for and against what is proposed in the question.
► Think what central argument you would use to structure your essay.

TOPIC OUTLINE

1815–22 Lord Liverpool and the issue of public disorder and government repression

Reasons for large-scale public discontent include:

► Economic dislocation after the war, with rapid demobilization of the army and navy and the end of war demand before traditional European markets had recovered; poor harvests aggravated this.
► Government policies have been seen as both repressive of discontent (Gag Acts, suspension of Habeas Corpus, use of military to deal with uprisings, backing the actions of the Peterloo magistrates) and in themselves reactionary and contributing to the discontent (Corn Laws introduced, income tax abolished and replaced by duties on goods).

It is easy to spend too long in essays on describing outbreaks of discontent. It is more important to prepare a reasoned assessment of the political measures taken by Liverpool's government. Note:

► Liverpool represented the landed interest in the state, which was concerned to maintain law and order and had fearful memories of the French Revolution.
► He had few resources other than the military to maintain law and order.

It is now common to see his many problems as explaining his apparently repressive actions and he needs to be judged by what was possible for government at the time. It was an age of *laissez-faire* and it will not do simply to assert that he should have introduced reforms, though the few modest attempts at reform before 1822 should be acknowledged.

1822–27 Lord Liverpool and the Liberal (Enlightened) Tories

An issue commonly raised in history examinations is how far Tory policies and government changed in 1822. There were certainly new men promoted to cabinet posts – Peel, Huskisson, Robinson and Canning, though all had started their political careers in the earlier period, and reforms rather than repression seemed to mark the second phase of Liverpool's period in power. Reforms included:

► reductions in the number of capital offences (Peel)
► gaol reforms (Peel)
► repeal of the Combination Acts
► removal of trade restrictions and some relaxation of customs duties (Huskisson).

There were however no constitutional reforms until after Liverpool had gone. The earlier repression was less needed as the economy recovered and discontent died down. In many ways the continuity across 1822 is worth stressing and the limits of Tory 'liberalism' need identifying. At this point it is also important to prepare an overall assessment of Liverpool's political achievement. He was certainly in office for a long time.

1827–30 Disintegration of the Tories

This may not often figure as an examination topic but it is essential background to questions on the 1832 reform of the parliamentary system. The personal antagonisms after Liverpool's death and, above all, the emergence of the Catholic

Emancipation issue which he had so skilfully contained, led to a split in the Tory Party which enabled the Whigs to do well in the 1830 election and to form a government, opening a new phase in political history. Note that after Liverpool's departure two important reform measures were introduced:

▶ 1829 formation of the Metropolitan Police Force, the work of Peel
▶ 1829 Catholic Emancipation, in which Peel again played a central, controversial role.

1830–32 The Whigs and the passing of the 1832 Parliamentary Reform Act

The defects of the unreformed parliamentary system need to be understood but usually only to be in a position to assess how many of them were removed by the 1832 Act and to appreciate what remained unchanged. Few exam questions expect a descriptive account of alleged defects.

▶ Why it was possible to pass an Act in 1832 is a common question. This involves detailed knowledge, which needs adapting to specific questions, both of the build-up of pressure for reform and the details of how the measure passed through parliament in 1831–32.
▶ The Whig motives in pushing through the reform are a separate important topic.

An assessment of what the Act achieved is essential; this should include consideration of why so many radicals remained unsatisfied by the changes introduced.

1833–41 Whig governments and their later reforms

The Whig government's reforms, coming mainly in the years 1833–36 with a subsequent loss of momentum, dealt with major social problems. Together they constitute a formidable reform record, often leading to the 1830s being labelled 'a decade of reform'. An overall assessment of the nature of this reform achievement is essential for any student of this topic. In examinations involving questions on separate nineteenth-century social issues you will also need a more detailed assessment of what the Whigs achieved in each of their reforms. These should be related to the gravity of the problems they faced. The main areas of social reform included:

▶ 1833 abolition of slavery in the British Empire
▶ 1833 first government education grant to schools
▶ 1833 first effective factory law providing for inspection of child labour in textile mills
▶ 1834 Poor Law Amendment Act, one of the great administrative reforms of the century
▶ 1835 Municipal Reform Act, reorganizing town government
▶ 1836 compulsory registration of births, marriages and deaths.

The nature of the problem faced, and the success of the legislation in meeting that problem, need, in each case, to be identified. The appropriate depth will depend on the nature of past questions on the topic.

1829–46 Assessing the political career of Sir Robert Peel

Peel's career in the Liverpool government pre-1827 needs to be borne in mind but is less important, in examination terms, than his work in and after 1829. This opened with his central controversial role in carrying Catholic Emancipation and his opposition to the 1832 Reform Act. The major examination topics then relate to

▶ his success, or otherwise, in building up a new 'Conservative' Party around the Tamworth Manifesto

▶ the achievements of his 1841–46 ministry, particularly in the field of economics
▶ his controversial role in the repeal of the Corn Laws and the effect of this on his 'new' party.

1838–46 Repeal of the Corn Laws

Introduced by Liverpool in 1815 to protect farmers and landowners from foreign grain imports, the Corn Laws became a major political issue from the late 1830s, when manufacturers and merchants formed the Anti-Corn-Law League to press for their repeal as harmful to the economy and raising food prices.

▶ The role of the League in achieving reform in 1846 is one important topic.
▶ Peel's conversion to repeal and his government carrying it is an important aspect of any assessment of his political career.

The crisis of 1846, involving the appalling famine in Ireland, Peel's conversion to repeal, the split in the Conservative Party and its consequent almost thirty years without a Commons majority take the subject forward. The economic results of repeal, however, were something of an anti-climax.

1838–48 Chartism

This working-class movement for political reform provides a usefully self-contained examination topic but you do need to understand the effects of the 1832 Parliamentary Reform Act on the political system; only then do the demands of the Chartists, and the reasons for their failure, make sense. The range of examination questions available to examiners is limited but includes

▶ both the economic and the political reasons for the rise of Chartism
▶ why people became Chartists
▶ the reasons for the Chartist failure to obtain further measures of political reform from parliament.

1846–68 Parliamentary instability

This is a difficult period for which to select revision topics. Many candidates avoid answering questions here, unless they are on Palmerston and foreign policy, preferring to move on to the more stable ministries after 1868.

▶ The reasons why there were so many minority and/or short-lived governments provide one topic, with the split in the Conservatives and the existence of the short-lived Peelite group central to any explanation.
▶ The Peelites also provide a way into questions on the emergence of the Liberal Party in this period, though explanations of this need to include commentary on social trends, like the development of urban middle-class politics away from Westminster.
▶ These topics in turn involve a useful reminder to know enough about the careers of Gladstone and Disraeli in these years to provide ideas and information for post-1868 questions.
▶ The 1867 Parliamentary Reform Act also provides useful insights on Gladstone and Disraeli as well as forming a natural bridge with the wider topic of parliamentary reform across the century.

Social and economic issues

The depth of study needs to be linked to the types of questions encountered in past papers. Topics on which questions are frequently asked, even in outline papers, include the following.

Poverty

The causes and incidence of poverty are part of the economic background of Britain emerging as the world's first urban industrial state. Do not get too bogged down in descriptive material. The central aspect of this topic is the passing of the 1834 Poor Law Amendment Act. It was more concerned with efficient administration of poor relief than with ending poverty, which was beyond the scope of nineteenth-century government.

Examination questions are often set on:

▶ the nature and extent of the pre-1834 Poor Law crisis
▶ the purpose, philosophy and terms of the 1834 Act
▶ how the post-1834 system worked and what it achieved
▶ how cruel the 1834 Act was and how new attitudes to poverty began to emerge only in the last two decades of the century.

In special topic papers you will need far more detail than for the overall assessments asked for in outline papers. The 1834 Act is also important for any assessment of the Whig reform achievement in the 1830s.

Public health

There is a danger in acquiring too much information on sanitary horrors. Opportunities to use this in examination questions are limited. There are more important issues for examiners:

▶ Analysing the emergence of pressure for public health reform in the 1830s and 1840s, with Edwin Chadwick providing a starting-point.
▶ The 1848 Public Health Act as the central sanitary legislation, including its impact on the sanitary problems and why it came so relatively late in the day, long after Poor Law reform for example.

It is worth taking this topic through to the great codifying measure, the 1875 Public Health Act.

Education

It is important to study this topic through to 1914.

▶ The first steps in the churches providing schools and in state involvement in education came in this period but the great legislative measures came in the period 1870–1902.
▶ You need to do more than just learn the terms of legislation and be able to assess how education, particularly of working-class children, improved across the century; the limits on improvement need to be borne in mind.

The 1870 Education Act is probably the most important single piece of legislation and the 1833 Whig education grant the most useful starting-point.

Factory reform

It is the early legislation that attracts most examination interest, the 1833 Factory Act and the 1842 Mines Act in particular. The opposition to reform in this area and the reasons for it, as well as the difficulties in implementing reforms, often appear as examination topics. Legislation on child-labour was central and, in assessing the impact on the lives of children, do not only remember the associated growth of working-class education but also reflect on the vast numbers of children who were, for decades, outside the scope of any legislation.

The railway network

In full-blown economic history papers there are many economic topics which form the basis of examination questions but railways are the most common nineteenth-century economic topic in general papers, with only questions on free trade to rival them. Too many candidates learn up an all-purpose railways answer which they then vaguely try to adapt to the specific terms of this year's question. Unless the terms of the question lend themselves to your range of ideas and knowledge, be wary. Common questions include

▶ the economic or the social consequences (they are not the same thing) of the creation of a railway network
▶ railway technology, in relation to both the construction and the running of the network.

Religion and society

Questions on religion require as much specific knowledge as those on any other topic. Do not assume that you can bluff your way to an answer but, if necessary, look elsewhere. Be prepared for questions on the following themes:

▶ Religious issues causing major political crises, notably over Catholic Emancipation (1829) and in the later history of Ireland.
▶ Religious belief encouraging humanitarian reforms. Look up the work of Lord Shaftesbury as the clearest example and the work of the Churches as the early providers of education to the working class (though later their rivalry often impeded progress).
▶ How religious was Victorian Britain? Be ready to illustrate how religious belief inspired individuals and how religious values dominated the lives of the middle class but be able to comment at some length on the findings of the 1851 Religious Census (the only one ever held) which showed how remote most of the working class, especially in the towns, were from religion. There is also the related issue of Victorian hypocrisy in various fields.

Useful information

Important terms

You should make sure, from your notes and textbooks, that you understand the following terms and feel able to use them confidently in your own writing: franchise, free trade, *laissez-faire*, liberal, radical, reactionary, repressive, poor relief, suffrage.

Important figures

Be ready to comment on or assess the careers of the following political figures: Lord Liverpool, Sidmouth, Castlereagh, Peel, Huskisson, Canning, Wellington, Grey, Melbourne, Russell, Palmerston, Gladstone, Disraeli, Lord Derby. Also know about the social reformers: Chadwick, Shaftesbury, Bentham (philosopher).

Statistics

1 Population of England, Scotland and Wales   1801   11 million
                                                              1831   16 million
                                                              1851   21 million

2 Number of voters pre-1832 around 450,000; after the 1832 Reform Act around 700,000.

★ REVISION ACTIVITY

The career of Lord Liverpool and the Liberal Tories to 1830

(a) List the main examples of government repression in the 1815–22 period.
(b) List the main examples of government reform activity in the 1822–27 period.

(c) Argue (one side of A4 paper maximum) that 1822 marked a great turning-point in British political life. Do not go into detail, simply refer to the lists above to provide supporting examples.

(d) Prepare an essay plan, ideas and information, to be used as the basis for an essay arguing that continuity across from 1822 to 1827 was far more important than any change of direction in 1822. This is not just a game proving that historians will believe and argue anything! Its aim is to get you to realize that history examinations are about problems; in this case it could be a question like:

How far do you agree that Lord Liverpool's government from 1815 to 1827 underwent a sharp change in direction in 1822?

The form of the question calls for a balanced answer:

1 You agree that it changed in certain ways.

2 Indicate, one sentence each, some examples.

3 In other ways continuity was more important.

4 Again indicate one sentence examples.

To do really well in a history examination you must provide a direct answer to the question. Your historical information will simply support your argument. Never just tell the tale of what Liverpool did before and then after 1822.

Now write a concluding paragraph, of not more than ten lines, summarizing what you feel about the issue of continuity and change in 1822. Remember the form of the question 'How far do you agree . . .' so you can give a balanced verdict *but* you must give a verdict that comes right back to the terms of the question asked.

(e) The Liberal Tories: list their reforms from 1822 to 1830, then list the issues they left untouched. Prepare an essay plan on whether they deserve the title 'Liberal Tories'. To do this at all well you will have to define (briefly!) what you understand by 'Liberal Tory' in the 1820s. Do this first.

Other revision ideas

Following the same lines as the work on Lord Liverpool, other revision ideas could include these topics:

Parliamentary reform

Prepare an essay plan for the question 'Why was a Parliamentary Reform Act passed in 1832?' (avoid spending long on describing the defects of the pre-1832 system; offer both long- and short-term reasons).

Robert Peel

List his main achievements after 1830 but then list also the points you would make in arguing that his career, both as party leader and as Prime Minister, was not totally successful.

Chartism

Write the opening paragraph of an essay examining the reasons for the failure of Chartism to win political reforms. Then write the concluding paragraph of the same essay. After completing this task read the essay on Chartism in the Part III answers section (pp. 66–8).

Politics after 1846

Draw up a list of the points you can use to explain why there was government instability at Westminster in the period 1846–59: turn those points into an essay plan.

General revision

Draw up a list of the main politicians of the period and note what points you would want to make in assessing their careers.

Essay plans

1 'Peel first created, then destroyed the Conservative Party.' Discuss.   (*25 marks*)
2 Why did so many working-class men become Chartists?   (*25 marks*)

Draw up a list of the points you intend to make in answering these essays. The plans should be lists of general points you wish to make in answering the questions. They should *not* be lists of historical facts.

PRACTICE QUESTIONS

Essay questions

Question 1
How far do you agree that it was disappointment at the terms of the 1832 Parliamentary Reform Act which led to the emergence of Chartism?

Question 2
'A great reforming ministry': examine this comment on the Whig reforms from 1833 to 1841.

Document question

Question 3 – 1832 Reform Act
Read the extract which follows and then consider how you might answer the questions below.

> Well then what is to be done? This. As we know there exists a House of Lords possessed by a spirit of unrelenting and incurable Toryism. . . . the present House of Commons is but slightly attached to Lord Grey's Administration and may any day in the week be induced to trip it up on some question unconnected with reform, under such circumstances Great Britain ought to exhibit . . . a determination not to endure for one moment the transfer of power from a Liberal to a Tory Cabinet. . . . a spirit must be manifested by the country as will render the early formation of a Tory Government politically impossible: second such an organisation of the whole constituency throughout the United Kingdom ought to be completed, without losing another week, as may secure the return of a large and upright majority in the reformed House of Commons, thus rendering the creation of a subsequent Tory Cabinet . . . impracticable. We repeat our solicitations . . . to our brethren the electors of Great Britain and Ireland, entreating them to organise and not to rest until the work be accomplished, election committees in every quarter, for the effectual return to the approaching Parliament of candidates in the interest of the people. . . . Let men be sought who will vote through fire and water for a redress of all practical grievances.
>
> (*Original Source*: editorial in *The Times* 12 June 1832)
> (*Reproduced in*: Smith, EA, *Reform or Revolution,*
> *A Diary of Reform in England 1830–1832*, Alan Sutton, 1992)

(a) What is meant in this extract by (i) 'Lord Grey's Administration' (ii) 'a subsequent Tory cabinet'?   (*2*)
(b) What can be inferred from the extract as to the attitude of *The Times* to the reform of parliament?   (*3*)
(c) What is the purpose of *The Times* in this editorial and how effectively does the language and tone of the article help promote that purpose?   (*5*)
(d) From your own knowledge, and using as appropriate the evidence in this extract, how far do you agree that pressure from outside parliament was largely responsible for the passing of the 1832 Reform Act?   (*15*)

(*Total marks 25*)

2 British domestic history 1868–1914

REVISION TIPS

Draw up a list of appropriate political revision topics in chronological order, for example:

► Gladstone's 1868–74 ministry
► Disraeli's 1874–80 ministry
► Ireland 1868–1914
► Conservative dominance 1886–1905
► The rise of the Labour Party to 1914
► The Liberal government 1906–14
► The fight for women's rights, particularly the right to vote

Social history themes arising from the growing concern with poverty can usefully link with the rise of the Labour Party and with the Liberal welfare measures from1906 as well as providing useful exam topics in their own right. Social history questions, except on poverty and the development of education, seem to be much less common in this period on outline papers than they were for the early nineteenth century, when the pioneer reform measures were being introduced. See the topic outline on British foreign policy 1815–1914 for other important revision topics (pp. 30–3). If you intend to revise Britain's role in the origins of the First World War then you will also find the map located in the topic outline on European history 1870–1914 a useful starting-point (p. 51).

Once more you need to revise through problem-solving and not just through factual recall. Such revision, by identifying historical problems, will in any case help you sort and classify your historical knowledge in a more easily memorable form. Examples of problems can include

► Why has Gladstone's 1868–74 ministry been generally regarded as one of the great reforming ministries of the nineteenth century?
► Is Disraeli better seen as a great domestic reformer or as a great empire builder and international statesman?
► Why was it so difficult, between 1868 and 1914, for the British parliament to solve the 'Irish question'?
► Why did a working-class political party (the Labour Party) emerge in the late nineteenth and early twentieth centuries?
► How far did the Liberal social reforms between 1906 and 1914 amount to a revolution in attitudes to welfare?

TOPIC OUTLINE

Gladstone's 1868–74 ministry

► Be prepared to explain Gladstone's political principles – religious commitment, strict morality, personal responsibility, government financial prudence, self-help – and to explain how these influenced his political work. These principles can easily be adapted into an analysis of the principles governing the British Liberal Party at this time and could be useful in regard to many different types of questions.

▶ List the legislation enacted by the ministry and have an opinion both on the problems it was designed to meet and how effective (and important) it was, for example:

1870 Education Act

Until 1870 governments had limited themselves to providing aid for church schools; now the state created local authorities, school boards, to fill the gaps where there were no church schools. It is the most important single action in creating an elementary (primary) school system and all the other late-nineteenth-century and twentieth-century extensions of education provision arise from it. Look up the details of the Act but also be ready to make an overall assessment of it on these general lines.

Other reforms and legislation

▶ You now need to form overall verdicts on the significance of Gladstone's other reforms, for example: army reforms, Civil Service reforms, University Tests Act, Trade Union Act and the Criminal Law Amendment Act (also about trade unions), Licensing Act, the Secret Ballot, Judicature Act. Remember to ask yourself what were the problems each was dealing with and how effectively the legislation met the problems, both in its detail and in its overall impact for the future.

▶ Then remember the very important Irish legislation. All of Ireland was part of the United Kingdom so, unless the question clearly excludes Ireland, such legislation is part of any answer on domestic reforms.

▶ Finally, in case you get a question on Gladstone's personal achievement or some other aspect of his life over a longer period, do remind yourself of his work prior to 1868, under Peel and as Chancellor of the Exchequer in the 1850s and 1860s.

Disraeli's 1874–80 ministry

As with Gladstone, look up Disraeli's earlier career in case there is a question which covers more than just this one ministry, in particular his early reform record – Young England, his social novel *Sybil*, his key role in carrying through the 1867 Second Parliamentary Reform Act, his brief 1868 ministry, his reform and imperialism speeches of 1872. Also important is his role in the split in the Conservative Party in 1846 and then his work, with Lord Derby, in holding the party together through from the aftermath of 1846 to forming a majority government in 1874. Any of this material may be added to an assessment of Disraeli's role after 1874 but not of course if the question quite clearly limits you to a discussion of the 1874–80 ministry for then it would be irrelevant.

Questions on the 1874–80 ministry

▶ often require a comparison of Disraeli as a domestic reformer with his work for the empire or in foreign affairs

▶ sometimes invite discussion of his limited reform achievement when set against his earlier interest in reform

▶ often require you to compare his reform record with that of Gladstone

▶ sometimes ask for an assessment of his legacy to the Conservative Party (where, irritatingly, you are occasionally required to contrast his work with that of Peel).

Comparative questions, involving the work of two major figures, can be vast and you will have to answer directly and economically. For the 1874–80 ministry useful topics to support an answer will include:

Domestic reforms

Artisans' Dwellings Act, Public Health Act, Factory Act, Sale of Food and Drugs Act, Merchant Shipping Act, Climbing Boys Act, Conspiracy and Protection of

Property Act, Employers and Workmen Act (the last two are trade union Acts). How much credit does Disraeli personally deserve for these reforms? Note that all of them occurred in the first year of the ministry and that the reforms then dried up. Was this really a programme of reform to make working-men vote Tory and did Disraeli have a policy of 'Tory democracy'? (Be ready to link this to his motives in carrying the 1867 Second Parliamentary Reform Act.)

Imperial and foreign affairs

Purchase of the Suez Canal shares; Victoria made Empress of India; military matters in South Africa and in Afghanistan (can Disraeli really be held responsible or was it men on the spot?); the Eastern Question and the Congress of Berlin, what did Disraeli achieve there? (remember to include acquiring Cyprus); Disraeli's imperial legacy to the Conservative Party.

Ireland 1868–1914

▶ Gladstone's attempts, in his 1868–74 and his 1880–85 ministries, to solve Irish religious and land grievances (especially the church legislation of 1869 and the Land Acts of 1870 and 1881): be ready to assess both his success and its limits.

▶ Gladstone and Home Rule – why he failed to bring it about in both 1886 and 1893 and (as a separate topic usually) the unfortunate effect of his Irish policies on the Liberal Party through to 1906.

▶ The Conservatives and Ireland 1886 to 1905 – firm government and few concessions.

▶ Third Home Rule Bill of 1912 – the problems it provoked in Ireland and why it never became law.

Look at past papers at this point for you have now set up the basic 'Irish issues' for taking this topic further. If your syllabus goes on to the 1921 division of Ireland between North and South it would be sensible to continue your revision through to that date, including of course the 1916 Easter Rising.

Conservative dominance 1886–1905

This period was dominated by Lord Salisbury, who was Prime Minister briefly in 1885–86, then from 1886 to 1892 and from 1895 to 1902. His nephew, Balfour, was then Prime Minister until the end of 1905. Examiners do ask political questions about this period but it is not popular with candidates and may be one to leave out of your revision schedule, but only after checking on past papers. Domestic topics are not numerous but include:

▶ The reorganization of local government (1888 Local Government Act).

▶ A minor social reform of 1897 allowing workers to claim compensation for injuries at work.

▶ An important Education Act in 1902 which gave control of schools to local authorities and created the basis for the secondary education system.

▶ The most important question may well be to ask why the Conservatives dominated the period and this involves close study of the problems facing the Liberals with Gladstone pressing Irish Home Rule, splitting the party and driving Joseph Chamberlain into the Conservative ranks. Chamberlain is a revision topic in his own right, and a more interesting one than Salisbury, but all of this theme should be extended to revise why the Liberals won the 1906 election. That is a very common examination question.

The main interest of the period lay in overseas affairs especially with the dramatic expansion of British rule in Africa culminating in the difficulties of the 1899–1902 Boer War. This in turn led to an important switch in foreign policy as Britain started to look for international allies (the Anglo-Japanese alliance of 1902).

The rise of the Labour Party to 1914

Most examination questions want to know why this occurred and may require you to assess how much progress the party had really made by 1914.

Essential background includes: the social problems of the working class in the late nineteenth century, the extensions of the franchise in 1867 and 1884 and the growth of the trade unions in the last decades of the century.

Factors involved in the rise of the Labour Party, which will need revision, are

► the emergence of socialist ideas and socialist organizations like the Social Democratic Federation, the Socialist League and the Fabian Society
► the part played by Keir Hardie and the foundation of the Independent Labour Party
► the role of the TUC and the establishment of the Labour Representation Committee in 1900
► the electoral progress of the party in 1906 and the two elections of 1910, including relations with the Liberal Party
► the strengths and weaknesses of the Labour Party in 1914.

The Liberal government 1906–14

There is a series of important examination topics under this general heading, including

► why the Liberals won the 1906 general election
► the parliamentary crisis of 1909 to 1911, the issues involved and how it was settled
► the Liberals and Irish Home Rule
► the Liberal welfare measures and how they changed the Victorian Poor Law (did they indeed lay the basis for the later Welfare State?)
► the build-up of international alliances and the reasons for Britain's entry into the First World War (see the topic outline on British foreign policy 1815–1914, pp. 30–3).

Each of these may well form a revision topic in its own right, though not more than one of them will appear in any one examination paper. If you are hoping for a question on the Liberals in this period the best advice is to cover them all and only then hope that your banker topic comes up.

The fight for women's rights, particularly the right to vote

Set your revision of the franchise issue in the wider context of the accepted role for women in society. Otherwise this topic doesn't make much sense. Remember women over 30 got the vote as late as 1918 and on equal terms with men only in 1928. Examination questions in this area usually want to know why the vote was not achieved by 1914.

You need to know about:

► the subservient role of women in the nineteenth century in terms of property and marriage, how this gradually changed but how Victorian attitudes remained deeply opposed to a political role for women (be able to quote the arguments of opponents, including many women)
► the ineffectiveness of the suffragists' (legal) pressure
► how, after 1900, the less legal tactics of the suffragettes proved ineffective in bringing pressure on the government and may even have hardened attitudes
► the role of the Pankhurst family
► how the First World War brought the vote that earlier political pressure had been unable to achieve (do take this topic through to 1918).

Useful information

Important terms

Make sure that you understand and can use the following correctly in your own writing: balance of power, collectivism, free trade, Home Rule, imperialist, jingoist, *laissez-faire*, nationalist, protectionism, socialism, tariff reform, welfare state.

Important figures

Be ready to assess the careers of the following major political figures: Asquith, Chamberlain (Joseph), Disraeli, Gladstone, Lloyd George, Parnell, Salisbury. Be prepared to comment on these less important, but still significant, figures: Balfour, Bonar Law, Campbell Bannerman, Randolph Churchill, Winston Churchill (to 1914), Keir Hardie, the Pankhursts, Cecil Rhodes. If you can place them in context, they could be very useful in adding credible and relevant detail to the argument and analysis in your essays.

REVISION ACTIVITY

Disraeli

(a) Write the opening paragraph of an essay arguing that Disraeli was more important as an imperialist than for his domestic reforms between 1874 and 1880.

(b) List the points you would want to make in the body of your essay, then turn these points into an essay plan. (Clearly you can argue the opposite theme if that is your view but you must have an opinion, for the essay is about an assessment of the themes and not just a description of them.)

Women

Make a list of the points you would want to make explaining why women did not get the vote by 1914. Put the list of points in a logical order to form an essay plan.

Other revision ideas

Time-chart

Construct an outline time-chart of the period 1868–1914 showing the major ministries and the dates of key events – do not at this stage put in any detail.

Liberal government

Make a detailed diagram of the issues to be considered in assessing the achievement of the Liberal government 1906–14.

Labour Party

Prepare your ideas explaining why the Labour Party emerged and developed in the years to 1914. How would you start an essay on this topic?

PRACTICE QUESTIONS

Essay questions

Question 1

Why is Gladstone's 1868–74 ministry so often described as a 'great reforming ministry'?

Question 2

How do you explain the scale of the Liberal victory in the 1906 general election?

3 British domestic history 1914–51

REVISION TIPS

Draw up an outline chronology of the period. It falls into quite distinct sections:

► 1914–18 Impact of the First World War on Britain
► 1919–39 Society and politics in the inter-war years
  – Dominance of the Conservative Party
  – Decline of the Liberals
  – First Labour governments
  – 1930s The Depression
  – 1930s Failure of political extremism
► 1939–45 Impact of the Second World War on Britain
► 1945–51 Record of the Labour government

Check carefully that all of the period falls within your examination syllabus. If your paper ends in 1939 then you must not waste time going beyond that date. It is also important to check past papers in order to see

► what the likely balance of questions will be across the period
► whether the paper is largely political or whether social issues also figure prominently
► whether there are foreign policy questions (if there are, consult the topic outline on British foreign policy 1914–70s, pp. 37–40).
► which topics seem to be favoured by those setting the examination paper.

There is a lot to cover so now draw up a revision strategy giving an order of priority. In the inter-war period many topics link together, for example the roles of the Conservative, Liberal and Labour parties, so speed up your revision by studying them as a bloc. The same material can often be adapted to very different questions. Check on the list of important figures (p. 27) but in each case think hard about how to use this biographical information to give more substance to likely examination questions.

The 1930s present revision difficulties. Domestic politics seem to provide fewer questions and the two best themes to revise could well be

► the impact of the economic depression on British society
► an analysis of British foreign and defence policy in the years leading up to the Second World War.

TOPIC OUTLINE

1914–18 Impact of the First World War on Britain

The actual fighting of the war will usually appear in papers on European history rather than British history. The war was the first in which all the resources of the state were totally committed to the fighting – the first 'total war' – and it is questions about the dramatic effect of this on society which appear in British history papers. You do however need to have a broad outline of how the war was fought if only to avoid obvious errors. The main areas to revise include economic, social and political effects.

Economic effects

These especially include the distortion of the economy and trade, including the loss of overseas investments, in order to fight the war and how this led to the post-war economic problems. It is the inter-war consequences which are most important in outline papers. The economic detail may be needed only by the few candidates who are taking economic history syllabuses but everyone should know the broad consequences.

Social effects

This comes down to how far life was different in the 1920s from how it had been pre-1914. You can consider the changed role of women in society, new social freedoms, new leisure opportunities, the decline of religion and the impact of the war's economic changes. Do not hold the war responsible for all the changes but be able to relate these to the war when relevant. If you study the social effects of the war at any length then you should certainly go on to study the social history of the 1930s and the Depression.

Political effects

These especially include how the pressures of conducting the war split, and so helped to destroy, the Liberal Party and how the role of women in the war helped gain them the vote in 1918 (of most value if you have studied this topic before 1914).

1919–39 Dominance of the Conservative Party

The topic could well be best opened up by preparing a time-chart on the inter-war career of Stanley Baldwin. You will need to be able to assess what made him such a formidable politician particularly in relation to

- ▶ 1926 General Strike (see the document question on p. 28)
- ▶ 1931 creation of the National Government
- ▶ 1936 Abdication Crisis
- ▶ his overall record as Prime Minister (1923–24, 1924–29, 1935–37).

Baldwin was the most important political figure of the inter-war years but remember also the general factors which favoured the Conservatives:

- ▶ the desire for political stability and the fear of communism among the middle classes and many 'respectable' members of the working class
- ▶ the influence of a predominantly right-wing press
- ▶ the weaknesses of the Liberal and Labour parties as opponents.

1919–39 Decline of the Liberals

The argument that the Liberals were in a critical state by 1914 is no longer generally accepted but you will need to be able to offer a brief comment on it (if your syllabus begins before 1914 then you will need to revise this issue more fully, for a question on Liberal decline could well stretch from pre-1914 to 1924 or 1929). The impact of the war was crucial, in causing the split between Asquith and Lloyd George, the two Liberal leaders. The effect of Lloyd George leading a Liberal–Conservative coalition government (1918–22) was also important. There were then many general factors:

- ▶ The war undermined many Liberal principles like free trade and belief in minimum government interference in society and the economy.

▶ The rise of the new working-class Labour Party (have some details) affected Liberal electoral support with its apparently greater relevance to post-war issues.
▶ The flight of middle-class voters and Liberal supporters to the Conservatives as a better protection against left-wing extremism.
▶ The collapse of the Liberal base in local government.
▶ The traditional fate of third parties in the British electoral system came into play after 1924 and is best illustrated from the 1929 election statistics.

(See the unsatisfactory student answer in Part III (pp. 73–4), but more for how *not* to organize an essay than for any value it has in revising this topic.)

1919–39 First Labour governments (the rise of the Labour Party)

Rehearse the reasons for the growth of the Labour Party. You will need to study the pre-1914 growth to understand later developments; questions may well reach across from before 1914 through to 1924. The First World War transformed the party's prospects: it

▶ gravely weakened the Liberals
▶ led to the 1918 extension of the franchise from which the working class chiefly benefited
▶ encouraged the growth of trade unionism on which Labour organization and finances rested
▶ ensured that post-war issues were largely economic and that Labour economic policies seemed more suited to post-war conditions than the older ideas of the Liberals.

Questions regularly occur on the achievements of the two inter-war Labour governments (1924 and 1929–31). Often the questions invite an explanation of why the governments did not achieve more. For this you will need to

▶ examine the party's status as a minority government after the general elections of December 1923 and 1929
▶ be able to comment in depth on the financial and political crisis that the second government faced in 1931
▶ explain why it found acceptable solutions very difficult to find.

Your essays on the Labour governments will have more substance if you can comment on the roles of MacDonald and Snowden and also examine Labour policy and actions. The 1931 crisis led into the formation of the National Government and it would need very little extra work to be ready for a question on this topic. Assessing the subsequent achievements of the National Government, to 1935 or 1939, is a different topic and not one about which questions are very frequently asked.

1930s The Depression

Questions here most commonly relate to the effect of the Depression on the lives of ordinary people. In assessing this it will be useful to

▶ be able to explain how the Depression arose (economic and financial origins from 1929 to 1931)
▶ be able to quote some unemployment statistics for the early 1930s
▶ cite and comment on some of the hardships endured, including the limited help available from public relief (the application of the controversial 'means test' is central to this)
▶ refer to which industries and which areas were most seriously affected (be ready to offer a thorough geographic survey of the United Kingdom)
▶ explain why the National Government could do so little to improve the economy.

Be prepared to demonstrate, and argue at some length, that all was not doom and gloom. Be able to refer to growth industries and relatively prosperous regions. For those in work there were new leisure opportunities, new housing prospects and new household goods. It often depended on where you lived and worked as to how you fared (be ready for a question on these lines). Have available an explanation of how recovery spread in the late 1930s on the back of new industries, housing growth and the beginnings of rearmament.

1930s Failure of political extremism

This is not as common a political examination topic as are questions on one or more of the three main political parties. It is, however, quite self-contained and easily covered. There are general reasons why extremists did not do as well in Britain as in other European countries:

▶ Working-class voters remained loyal to the Labour Party.
▶ Baldwin proved an effective and reassuring right-wing leader within the democratic tradition and this prevented any large-scale drift of middle-class voters to fascism.
▶ The Depression was never as bad in Britain as it was in Germany.
▶ The loyalty of the army, the police and most of the great capitalists to the state was never in doubt.
▶ The internal weaknesses of the British fascists were many.

You will then need to be able to comment on the role of Mosley and the fascists in the 1930s and relate this to their failure to create a solid basis of support.

1930s British foreign policy

This important examination topic is dealt with in the separate topic outline on British foreign policy 1914–70s (pp. 37–9).

1939–45 Impact of the Second World War on Britain

The effects of fighting the Second World War on British society have attracted much attention from historians and examiners. The commitment to the war was total and it had a crucial impact on all aspects of life. If you hope to answer a question on this topic you will need to revise the economic, social and political effects.

Economic effects
There was an economic impact on industry, capital investment, the export trade, shipping, the sale of overseas investments, the direction of labour, including conscription, the control of resources including rationing, the running-down of the economic and transport infrastructure.

Social effects
These effects included the evacuation of children, the loss of housing through bombing, rationing, conscription and direction of labour, all leading to the growth of a general feeling that things had to be better after the war than they had been before. A useful starting-point for this would be to study both the terms and the impact of the Beveridge Report.

Political effects
The political consequences included, from 1940, a coalition government and led to the Labour Party victory in the 1945 election. This election on its own is a frequent examination topic.

1945–51 Record of the Labour government

Aspects that need revision certainly include the following:

▶ Why Labour won the 1945 election so overwhelmingly.
▶ Labour welfare proposals and the creation of the Welfare State – link this up with the war experience and with earlier reforms back to the 1906–14 Liberals. Be able to discuss the impact on the lives of ordinary Britons, what problems were being met and how successfully.
▶ The economic problems facing the post-war government.
▶ The programme of nationalization in both political and economic terms.
▶ Labour foreign policy and the origins of the Cold War.
▶ Why Labour lost the 1951 election.

Useful information

General elections

▶ 1918 – coalition government with Lloyd George as PM
▶ 1922 – Conservative governments led first by Bonar Law and then by Baldwin
▶ 1923 – first Labour government, under Ramsay MacDonald, formed in January 1924
▶ 1924 – Conservative government under Baldwin
▶ 1929 – MacDonald's second Labour government
▶ 1931 – MacDonald's recently formed National Government returned
▶ 1935 – National Government re-elected, Baldwin became PM (Chamberlain 1937); coalition government formed under Churchill in 1940; ten-year gap between elections
▶ 1945 – sweeping Labour victory, Attlee PM
▶ 1950 – precarious Labour majority
▶ 1951 – Conservative victory, Churchill PM (until 1955)

Important terms

Make sure you understand and can use the following terms: balance of power, coalition government, economic depression, franchise, general strike, means test, pacifism.

Important figures

You should be able to assess the work of the following: Asquith, Lloyd George, Baldwin, Macdonald, Chamberlain, Churchill, Mosley, Attlee, Bevin.

★ REVISION ACTIVITY

Politics between the wars

Remember that this topic is taken to illustrate the type of revision activity that can be adapted for use with other topics on which you hope to answer exam questions.

(a) List the general elections from 1918 to 1935 and note any significant features of the results with regard to the effect on each of the political parties. If your knowledge is, at this stage, quite vague, consider turning this into a time-chart of ministries (their leading personnel, problems and achievements) and elections from 1918 to 1951.
(b) Prepare an essay plan to explain why the Liberal–Conservative coalition government collapsed in 1922.
(c) Write the opening paragraph of an essay explaining why the National Government was set up in 1931.

(d) Write the concluding paragraph of an essay explaining why the Conservative Party were so dominant in politics between the wars.

Other revision ideas

First World War and society
Draw up a list of headings on how the First World War affected British society. Was the war really an 'engine for change'?

Social opportunities in the 1930s
How would you answer a question proposing that the 1930s, far from being a period of terrible distress among the working class, was one of great social opportunities for many among them? Prepare a plan to answer this essay question.

Labour victory 1945
'It was the experience of fighting the Second World War that led to the Labour victory in the 1945 election.' How far do you agree? List the points you would want to make in answering this question. In particular work out what balance you will strike on 'How far you agree' in your final paragraph. Could you carry out this activity as part of an informal group discussion? The examination is not competitive and sensible cooperation could improve all your marks.

PRACTICE QUESTIONS

Essay questions

Question 1
Examine the view that fighting the First World War, rather than events after the war, brought about the end of the British Liberal Party. (Draw up your own plan to provide a clear-cut answer before turning to the student answer in Part III.)

Question 2
How successful was the Labour government from 1945 to 1951 in solving the economic problems it encountered? (List the points you want to make before turning to the essay plan in Part III.)

Document question

Question 3 – the 1926 General Strike

Extract I

There are two distinct issues, the stoppage in the coal industry and the general strike. The stoppage in the coal industry has followed nine months enquiry and negotiations. I did my utmost to secure agreement on the basis of the Commission's report and I shall continue my efforts to see that in any settlement justice is done both to the miners and the owners. What then is the issue for which the government is fighting? It is fighting because while negotiations were still in progress the Trade Union Council ordered a general strike, presumably to try to force Parliament and the community to bend to its will . . . I am a man of peace . . . but I will not surrender the safety and security of the British Constitution.

(Part of a speech by Stanley Baldwin in May 1926)

Extract II

We are as firm in our belief that there was no other course open to us as the Prime Minister is firm in his. We believe that this course was taken not by anti-patriots, not by people who wanted a revolution. . . . On the Labour side I do not disguise that there are people who (would) welcome this . . . but they are an insignificant minority. I have never disguised that, in a challenge to the Constitution, God help us unless the Government won. . . . But this is not a revolution. It is merely a plain economic industrial dispute where the workers say 'We want justice'.

(Part of a speech by J H Thomas, trade union leader, in May 1926)

(a) Explain what, in the context of these extracts, you understand by 'the general strike'. (2)

(b) (i) What was Baldwin's purpose in making the speech which is extract I? (3)
   (ii) In what ways and how effectively does Baldwin in extract I seek to win the support of his audience? (5)

(c) On what issues and how widely do the speakers in these two extracts differ in their interpretation of the 1926 crisis? (5)

(d) In the light of your own knowledge how full an account of the issues at stake in the General Strike of 1926 can be constructed from these extracts? What light do the extracts throw on the reasons for the failure of the strike? (10)

(*Total marks 25*)

Attempt to answer these sub-questions, which are intended to give practice in reading and interpreting document evidence. Then turn to the answers suggested in Part III (p. 75).

4 British foreign policy 1815–1914

✓ REVISION TIPS

This vast topic can usefully be divided into several largely self-contained sections:

▶ Issues in nineteenth-century British foreign policy
▶ 1812–27 Castlereagh and Canning
▶ 1830–41 Palmerston's early foreign policy
▶ 1841–46 Aberdeen Foreign Secretary
▶ 1846–65 Palmerston's later foreign policy
▶ 1874–80 Disraeli's foreign and imperial policy
▶ 1900–14 New alliances and the drift to war

It would be more sensible to revise just those sections in which you are particularly interested, provided of course that, in past papers, they appear also to interest the examiners. Popular topics include

▶ Castlereagh and Canning, Foreign Secretaries from 1812 to 1827, on whom comparative questions are very common.
▶ Palmerston's conduct of foreign policy from 1830 to 1841, 1846 to 1851, 1855 to 1865 – questions on Palmerston often run to 1841 or on from 1846 but, in terms of exam tactics, it would be wise to revise both periods or neither.
▶ The principles on which the conduct of foreign policy was based through from 1815 (the Vienna Peace Settlement) and how effective Castlereagh, Canning and Palmerston were in forwarding Britain's international interests.
▶ The nature of Britain's foreign policy interests – establishing these could be invaluable in provided essay structures and criteria for assessing the work of individuals. You should at the same time consult the political map of Europe in the nineteenth century, in the topic outline on European history 1815–70 (p. 42), and be able to use it to comment on British foreign policy.
▶ The Crimean War is well worth revising if it is also likely to appear in a European paper.
▶ Gladstone's foreign policy, however, rarely appears as a question standing on its own. Revise it largely to flesh out an overall assessment of his 1868–74 ministry. Note that Ireland was within the UK and so is a domestic topic.
▶ Disraeli's achievements in foreign and imperial policy often appear by inviting comparison with his domestic reputation as a social reformer. You should revise the domestic, imperial and foreign aspects of his 1874–80 ministry.
▶ The new direction in foreign policy from 1900 to 1914, as Britain entered into foreign alliances, with the period culminating in its entry into the First World War, is a sensible topic to revise, especially if you are also studying the same period in European history.

◎ TOPIC OUTLINE

Issues in nineteenth-century British foreign policy

In commenting on foreign policy some general points can have relevance in quite different questions, for example:

- From 1815 the supremacy of the Royal Navy gave Britain easily affordable security at home and also protected imperial trade routes.
- For much of the century Britain was the only world-wide imperial power.
- All this enabled successive Foreign Secretaries to assert British policies very firmly, Palmerston being particularly noted for this.
- It was in Britain's interest to ensure that no one power came to dominate continental Europe. In 1815 this made it suspicious of France, later it made for hostility to any hint of Russian expansion. This 'balance of power' in Europe was the main principle guiding policy after 1815.
- From 1870 this easy security became more difficult to maintain following the creation of the German Empire, though British statesmen like Gladstone and Disraeli were slow to perceive what was happening.

The changes became inescapable at the end of the nineteenth century, with Britain's international isolation cruelly exposed in the Boer War (1899–1902) and the German programmes of heavy battleship building (1898 onwards) posing a serious threat to the security of the British Empire. At this point British foreign policy began to move in new directions.

1812–27 Castlereagh and Canning

A full assessment of Castlereagh's term as Foreign Secretary should include his important work in holding together the Allied coalition which by 1815 had defeated Napoleon. Assessing his work in this period of war may well amount to half of any assessment of his full career as Foreign Secretary. Many foreign policy questions start in 1815, however, with the end of the Napoleonic War and with the calling of the Vienna Peace Conference. The precise terms of the question will decide whether the 1812 to 1815 period is relevant, so take care.

Castlereagh
Revise both the Vienna Peace Settlement, including his view of the formation of the Holy Alliance, the formation of the Quadruple Alliance and the origins and work of the Congress System through to his suicide in 1822.

- What was he trying to achieve?
- What principles underlay his work?
- How successful was he?

The most common question on this topic is to be asked to compare the work of Castlereagh and Canning. An effective answer is likely to be along the lines that they had much in common in terms of protecting British interests and in maintaining a balance of power and peace in Europe. It was circumstances and presentation that changed – not fundamentals. Canning did not have Castlereagh's long association with European statesmen and problems and he was also prepared to assert Britain's interests more firmly.

Canning
Be ready to comment on

- his work with the Congress System, which for all practical purposes came to an end during his period in office (though Castlereagh had earlier begun to detach Britain from it)
- his role with regard to checking French influence in Spain and in South America
- his policies towards the danger of Russian expansion towards the Eastern Mediterranean
- the issue of Greek independence and the actions he took
- the complications caused in the eastern Mediterranean by the French and Mehemet Ali.

Canning's principles (aims) and his effectiveness will have to come into any essay. It will never be enough merely to describe what happened or what Canning did.

1830–41 Palmerston's early foreign policy

As with earlier Foreign Secretaries you must be able to comment on Palmerston's aims (principles) and his effectiveness in upholding British interests. The main issues with which he had to deal in this period were

- ▶ 1830–31 Belgian independence
- ▶ 1834 Portuguese and Spanish pretenders
- ▶ 1839–42 Opium War against China
- ▶ The Eastern Question with the Treaty of Unkiar Skelessi (1834) and the Straits Convention (1841).

Ask yourself why each of these concerned Britain, check what Palmerston's policy was in each case and then form a one or two sentence verdict on his effectiveness on each occasion.

1841–46 Aberdeen as Foreign Secretary

This is too limited a topic for an individual question but remind yourself of his work to improve relations with France and the United States. This and his more conciliatory way of dealing with issues made a great contrast with Palmerston and you might get an exam question which spanned this period in which you could make and illustrate this point.

1846–65 Palmerston's later foreign policy

Palmerston was Foreign Secretary from 1846 to 1851 and for most of the 1855–65 period he was, as Prime Minister, the most important figure in deciding British foreign policy. He was, however, not involved in the British becoming involved in the 1854–56 Crimean War. Major foreign policy issues with which he was involved in these years included

- ▶ 1846 breach with France over the Spanish Marriages (contrast with Aberdeen)
- ▶ 1848 revolutions in many European countries
- ▶ 1850 Don Pacifico affair
- ▶ 1851 recognizing the future Napoleon III's extension of power as French President without consulting cabinet colleagues and for which he was dismissed
- ▶ 1856 the Arrow incident and bombardment of Canton
- ▶ 1859–60 events central to the unification of Italy
- ▶ 1861–65 the American Civil War (the Trent and the Alabama affairs)
- ▶ 1863 Polish Revolt, which he was unable to help
- ▶ 1864 Schleswig-Holstein affair, where he was unable to help the Danes against Prussia.

Palmerston died in 1865. For each of these later episodes you need to be able to provide a brief judgement on either Palmerston's manner of conducting foreign policy and/or its effectiveness in promoting British interests. Use these separate verdicts to construct an overall assessment of his record in foreign affairs. It seems likely that it will be a mixed verdict with the limits of Britain's ability to influence European continental events becoming more evident in the 1860s.

1874–80 Disraeli's foreign and imperial policy

Questions on this usefully self-contained period often require comparison of Disraeli's domestic and imperial/foreign policy achievements. The issues involved are considered in the topic outline on British domestic history 1870–1914 (pp. 18–22).

1900–14 New alliances and the drift to war

A useful starting-point is to note that the 1870 Prussian defeat of France and the consequent unification of Germany into one state created a very different political balance in continental Europe than had existed since 1815. Palmerston in the 1860s had been unable to dominate in the same way as earlier but the limits of British power were to become even more obvious towards the end of the century. The central foreign policy themes of these years are

▶ the pressures which persuaded Britain to move from isolating itself from continental entanglements to seeking alliances and understandings with other powers
▶ how these new links became strengthened and more difficult to evade in the first decade of the twentieth century
▶ how and why Britain in 1914 found itself drawn into the continental war against Germany and its allies.

The content of the topic outline on European history 1870–1914 will be particularly useful in revising British foreign policy in the years before the First World War. If you are also studying European history in the period to 1914 then this topic area, on British foreign policy, is an obvious one to revise. Do not expect a similar question on both European and British papers!

Useful information

Map
Make yourself familiar with the map of Europe in 1815 (placed in the topic outline on European History 1815–70, p. 42) and be aware of how the unification of Germany and also Italy, in the 1860s, changed it.

Important terms
Make sure that you understand and are able to use the following terms: arms race, balance of power, defensive alliance, entente, 'glorious isolation', imperialism, jingoism, national interests.

Important figures
Establish, from your notes and textbooks, that you understand and can assess the work in foreign affairs of the following: Castlereagh, Canning, Palmerston, Aberdeen, Gladstone, Disraeli, Lord Salisbury, Sir Edward Grey. Limit your research to figures from the period you are studying for the examination.

REVISION ACTIVITY

Castlereagh and Canning

(a) Construct a time-chart of the foreign policy issues which arose between 1815 and 1827. Take the issues in turn and think what each one tells you about the foreign policy aims and achievements of either Castlereagh or Canning.
(b) Draw up a plan for an essay examining whether Canning's foreign policy from 1822 to 1827 was more a continuation of Castlereagh's policies than it was a rejection of them.
(c) Write the opening paragraph of the essay explaining what theme you intend to follow in the answer.

(d) List the main events in foreign policy from 1815 to 1827 which you will refer to in the essay (be realistic as to how many you will have time to discuss in an examination answer).

Other revision ideas

Time-chart
Draw up a time-chart of the foreign policy events with which Palmerston was concerned from 1830 to 1841 and from 1846 to his death in 1865.

Palmerston
Assume that you have been asked to assess Palmerston's effectiveness in conducting British foreign policy, first from 1830 to 1841 and from 1846 onwards.

▶ How would you use each of the events on your time-chart in your assessment?
▶ What does each episode tell you about how he conducted foreign policy?
▶ What principles underlay his foreign policy?

PRACTICE QUESTIONS

Essay questions

Question 1
Explain why Britain entered into so many foreign policy obligations to other countries in the period 1902 to 1914. How far do you agree that these commitments made its entry into the First World War inevitable? (Spend at least ten minutes considering the points you would want to make in answering each part of this question, before turning to the student answer in Part III.)

Question 2
'Throughout the century from 1815 to 1914 it was relatively easy for Britain to secure its foreign policy objectives in Europe.' Discuss.

▶ Decide whether you would prefer to agree with this quotation or disagree with it.
▶ List the episodes you would mention in supporting your answer.
▶ Can you work out the beginnings of the opposite argument?
▶ Turn to the essay plan in Part III.

Document question

Question 3 – Palmerston's foreign policy

Extract I

I have desired the Admiralty to instruct Sir William Parker to take Athens on his way back from the Dardanelles and to support you in bringing at last to a satisfactory ending the settlement of our claims upon the Greek Government. He should of course begin by reprisals, that is by taking possession of some Greek property. . . . The next thing would be a blockade . . . of ports. . . . Of course Pacifico's claim must be fully satisfied.

(Letter from Palmerston to the British ambassador in Greece, 1849)

Extract II

The Greek [Pacifico] case has done more harm to Palmerston than any of his greater enormities. The other Ministers are extremely annoyed at it and at the sensation it has produced. The disgust felt at those bullying and worthless operations is great and universal and it will of course tend to make us more odious abroad. As far as Palmerston himself is concerned, he will as usual escape unscathed. He is so popular and . . . he is never at a loss, nor afraid nor discomposed.

(From the memoirs of Charles Greville, February 1850)

Extract III

A British subject, in whatever land he may be shall feel confident that the watchful eye on the strong arm of England will protect him against injustice and wrong.

(Part of Palmerston's speech to the House of Commons defending his conduct in the Don Pacifico affair, June 1850)

Extract IV

He has triumphed over the great mass of educated opinion, over . . . The Times, over two branches of the Legislature, over the Queen and the Prince and most of the Cabinet he sits in, besides all foreign nations.

(Lady Clarendon writing in her diary in June 1850 about the effects of Palmerston's Don Pacifico speech from which extract III is taken)

(a) What do you understand by 'Pacifico's claim' in extract I? (2)

(b) What can be established from these extracts about the ideas underlying Palmerston's foreign policy and about his methods in carrying that policy out? (5)

(c) From the evidence of these extracts alone, what can be said about Palmerston's popularity in 1850? (5)

(d) Note the origins of extracts II and IV and suggest some questions a historian might wish to ask about them in assessing the value of their evidence. (3)

(e) From the evidence of these extracts and on the basis of your own knowledge, consider the general lessons that the Don Pacifico affair might teach a historian about Britain's role in Europe in the mid-nineteenth century. (10)

(*Total marks 25*)

5 British foreign policy 1914–70s

✓ **REVISION TIPS**

The period divides naturally into an inter-war period from 1919 to 1939 and the post-war world from 1945. The Second World War itself was a pivotal time in British history but is not one much favoured by examiners of British history, except in domestic questions on the effects of the war on British society.

Inter-war period 1919–39

► Britain's international position at the end of the First World War
► The 1920s and stability
► The 1930s and appeasement
► Defence policy in the 1930s

Remind yourself of Britain's pre-eminent position in world affairs prior to 1914 and as controller of the world's greatest empire, and also how hard the country's economy had been hit by the First World War.

Look at a map of Europe in 1919 and the commentary on the pattern of European politics in the 1930s, both in the topic outline on European History 1914–45 (pp. 58–62).

The British Empire was at its territorial height in the 1920s but the first pressure was beginning to show:

► Understand how Britain's chief concern in the 1930s was not so much the rise of fascism in Europe but the question of how, in any future European war, Britain would be able to defend its overseas empire.
► The central foreign policy examination topic on the inter-war years is the policy of appeasement, practised particularly by the Chamberlain government from 1937. This is the most import revision issue from this topic area. It needs studying in its European setting.
► Revise the Churchill critique that appeasement was a betrayal of national interests, feeding Hitler's appetite for further territorial gains and also the more recent, contrary, view that Chamberlain had little choice but to pursue such a policy.

Post-war world from 1945
Britain was a junior partner of the United States in the Cold War against the Soviet Union. Post-1945 revision topics on British international policy include

► Britain's role in the early years of the Cold War, from 1945 to the Korean War (1950–53)
► The withdrawal from the British Empire 1947–70s
► European Union (the EEC or Common Market) to 1975.

The often reluctant moves towards a closer involvement with continental Europe are linked to the idea of a special relationship with the United States. This reached its climax in 1975 when the British people, in a referendum, voted two to one to join what became the European Union.

TOPIC OUTLINE

Britain's international position at the end of the First World War

This provides the setting for foreign policy until 1939. Note:

▶ the war strains on the economy, overseas investments and the increased National Debt

▶ Britain's central role at the Versailles Settlement and the work there of Lloyd George

▶ Britain's membership of the League of Nations and the absence of the United States

▶ world-wide imperial commitments, added to by the new mandates in Africa and the Middle East.

The 1920s and stability

This was a period of hopeful calm as Europe appeared to recover from the war and international relations became more stable. There are few examination questions directly on foreign policy at this time but note:

▶ 1922 Washington naval agreements with Japan, the USA, France and Italy

▶ Locarno Treaty (1925) and Kellogg-Briand Pact (1928)

▶ 1924 Labour government's recognition of the Soviet Union

▶ 1931 Statute of Westminster arranging full control of foreign policy for the 'white dominions' within the British Commonwealth, as it began to be called.

All these modest measures suggested worthwhile progress in international affairs generally but the Japanese attack on Manchuria in 1931 heralded a more turbulent era in which the limits of Britain's capacity any longer to act decisively in international relations were soon exposed. Foreign policy in the 1920s is valuable background to these new dangers though it may play little part in examination answers to specific questions.

The 1930s and appeasement

Almost all examination questions on British foreign policy in the 1930s revolve around the wisdom of the British and French governments attempting to appease Hitler, by making concessions to his demands in order to avoid war. You will need to be able to examine the arguments of both sides in the debate. It was Churchill, who in the 1930s had demanded that the government stood up to Hitler, and who, in his late 1940s *History of the Second World War*, launched what became the standard attack on the policy. Churchill argued:

▶ that it was evident from the outset that Hitler had a policy for Germany to dominate Europe

▶ that Hitler could have been checked by firm action opposing the remilitarizing of the Rhineland in 1936 or the union of Austria and Germany in 1938

▶ that the Czechs should have been backed to the point of war in 1938 at Munich – Chamberlain was seen as the villain here (this is the one European crisis that deserves in-depth study in case a question on it, alone, is asked in the examination paper)

▶ that Britain's defence capability should have been built up more rapidly.

You need to be able to give substance to this argument while avoiding accepting it uncritically.

Two major lines of attack on the Churchill thesis have emerged since the mid-1960s. First, the British historian A J P Taylor argued that Hitler did not have a master-plan for European domination and much of what happened occurred by chance. It was more difficult for the British government to see systematic German aggression than Churchill argued (you might add particularly without the benefit of hindsight).

Second, in the circumstances of the 1930s there was little alternative to a policy of buying peace by concessions; these circumstances included

▶ a strong pacifist feeling in Britain based on horror of what the next total war might bring
▶ concern that there were great social problems at home which deserved priority
▶ concern about the safety of the British Empire if a European war occurred
▶ the reluctance of the British Dominions to commit themselves to war
▶ the isolationism of the United States
▶ a feeling that some of Hitler's demands were not unreasonable given the harsh treatment Germany had received at Versailles
▶ deep distrust of the Soviet Union, the obvious ally against German expansionism, in British government circles. This bordered on a feeling that it was not a bad thing to have fascist Germany as a European bulwark against the spread of communism.

You need not only to develop this line of argument but also to add to it an examination of the contention that Churchill was such a maverick in British politics that it was reasonable in the 1930s for those of opposing views to discount his arguments and exaggerations. Preparing a brief paragraph on this theme, which if necessary could be expanded to essay length, will be a useful revision exercise.

Defence policy in the 1930s

The neglected state of Britain's defences constituted a second thrust of Churchill's charge against the British government and here Baldwin, prominent from 1931 to 1935 as deputy Prime Minister and then Prime Minister to 1937, was held responsible. It is worth noting that more was done than the government's critics allowed, particularly after 1935, in producing and developing plans to expand the number of fighter planes, to create an expeditionary force to fight on the continent and to build a radar shield around the south-east coastline. Churchill made mistakes here too, exaggerating German armaments and pressing for bombers, not fighters to be built.

Britain and the Second World War 1939–45

Examination questions on this topic almost always relate to the effect of the war on British society and link it with the Labour Party victory in the 1945 election. Questions on diplomatic and military aspects of the war are much less common in British history papers. Such topics have, however, included

▶ military questions on the importance of sea warfare or airpower in deciding the war
▶ examination of Britain's role in the final victory over Germany
▶ evaluation of Churchill's effectiveness as a war leader (which of course includes the diplomatic links he forged with Roosevelt and Stalin).

Britain's role in the early years of the Cold War, from 1945 to the Korean War (1950–53)

You will need to be able to set this topic in the context of the military and economic position in Europe at the end of the Second World War with much of Europe open to attack or infiltration by the Soviet Union. The new British Labour government was resolutely pro-American. Revision should include:

▶ the key roles played by Bevin, the Foreign Secretary, and Attlee, the Prime Minister, and also Churchill's dramatic 'Iron Curtain' speech in the United States

▶ the crucial episode, against communist infiltration in Greece, in which Britain drew the USA into a commitment to the defence of Western Europe

▶ Britain's role in later crises, the Berlin Airlift and the Korean War

▶ reintroduction of military conscription (National Service) from 1947 to 1962 and the costly rearmament programme from the late 1940s

▶ domestic impact of the Cold War commitment on the strained post-war economy and on the Welfare State

The withdrawal from the British Empire 1947–70s

This topic is part of the general withdrawal of European powers from their imperial role on which questions regularly appear in post-1945 world and European history papers. The main issues to revise with regard to Britain are

▶ impact of the Second World War on the British economy and on Britain's ability to continue defending the Empire

▶ emergence of the superpowers helping in bringing about withdrawal

▶ rise of nationalist movements in the colonies, also their encouragement by Japanese war victories in 1942

▶ loss of will in Britain to resist demands for independence

▶ chronology of decolonization from India in 1947 to the African and West Indian colonies in the 1960s and early 1970s

▶ the separate but not opposed roles of the Labour and Conservative parties in bringing about decolonization

▶ effect of the Suez adventure of 1956 on Britain's international status (this topic often attracts questions on both British and world history papers).

There are a limited number of questions which can be asked on this topic but be prepared for questions which are confined to either the Asian or the African colonies. Note also that in European or world history papers, questions regularly appear on the fate of the European empires in general. Be careful that the question is not limited to European *continental* countries but, if not, you should be able to cite the British experience as part of any wider answer on European decolonization.

European Union (the EEC or Common Market) to 1975

This topic requires some revision of the European context with the growth, in continental Europe, of the movement for closer cooperation, at first economically and then politically in the aftermath of the destruction of the Second World War and amid the tensions of the Cold War. If this topic falls within your European syllabus then the extra work to prepare for a British question should not be great. For a British question you will need to

▶ Draw up an outline chronology of Britain's moves with regard to the European Union, as it eventually became known, up to the referendum of 1975.

▶ Prepare an explanation of why so many Britons were reluctant to commit the country to involvement. The explanation needs to refer to insularity or patriotism, to not being invaded in war, to nostalgia for the imperial role and to the dream instead of a special relationship with the United States.

Useful information

Map
See the map of Europe after the 1919 Versailles Peace Settlement (in the topic outline on European history 1914–45, p. 58).

Important terms

Make sure that you understand and can use the following terms: appeasement, capitalism, communism, fascism, liberalism, Marxism, militarism, nationalism, Nazism, pacifism, socialism, totalitarianism, total war.

Important figures

Be in a position to comment on or assess the achievement of the following in foreign affairs: Lloyd George, Ramsay MacDonald, Chamberlain, Churchill, Attlee, Bevin, Eden.

REVISION ACTIVITY

Britain's international position after the Second World War

(a) List the main consequences of the Second World War in so far as they affected Britain's international role and foreign policy in the period to 1950.
(b) Draw up a time-chart of the chronology of Britain's withdrawal from its imperial commitments.
(c) Prepare an essay plan on 'Why, from 1945 to around 1970, did Britain abandon the vast majority of its imperial commitments?'
(d) List in sentence form the reasons why in the 1950s and 1960s so many Britons were reluctant to see their country enter the EEC.

Other revision ideas

European history

If you are also studying European history in the 1930s, bring your notes on European history and on British foreign policy together. Note the ways in which one might supplement the other but be careful in any examination that you answer the question set.

Churchill

List the reasons why, in the 1930s, Churchill was unable to command political attention. Prepare a plan for the following essay: 'With what justice can Churchill's career from 1930 to 1939 be regarded as "a study in failure"?'

PRACTICE QUESTIONS

Essay questions

Question 1

Examine the view that, from 1937 to 1939, appeasement of Hitler was a perfectly reasonable foreign policy for Chamberlain's government to pursue.

Question 2

How far do you agree that, in the Cold War period from 1946 to 1950, the British Labour government had little choice but to back the policies of the United States?

6 European history 1815–70

✓ REVISION TIPS

This period of European history is packed with possible examination topics so that careful selection of which topics to revise, is essential. It is commonly studied by candidates entered for a general outline paper and, as always, the best guide to revision is careful scrutiny of the recent past papers set by the examination board for which you are entered.

1814–15 Vienna Peace Settlement

There is an obvious starting-point with the political arrangements made at the 1815 Congress of Vienna at the end of the Napoleonic War; these are regularly set as an essay question.

▶ Study Map 1 on p. 42 and identify each of the great powers.
▶ Return to the map frequently during your revision of separate topics.

Other common exam topics

▶ 1815–70 France
  – 1815–30 Bourbon Restoration
  – 1830–48 Louis-Philippe
  – 1848–52 Second French Republic
  – 1852–70 Napoleon III and the Second Empire
  (To avoid a lottery you should revise French history across the period.)
▶ 1815–48 Repressive policies of Metternich (a complex international topic)
▶ 1848 Revolutions across Europe
▶ 1848–70 Unification of Italy
▶ 1848–70 Unification of Germany
▶ 1855–81 Reforms of Alexander II in Russia
▶ 1815–70 The Eastern Question (the study of this can usefully be taken through to 1914 as most questions on it will come after 1870).

Events in 1870 opened up a new period in international relations in Europe which culminated in the outbreak of the First World War in 1914. This later period is considered in the topic outline on European history 1870–1914 (pp. 52–5) but students taking an outline paper across the century need to make some strategic revision decisions about the spread of topics to revise, before going into detail either before or after 1870.

● TOPIC OUTLINE

1814–15 Vienna Peace Settlement

Examination questions concentrate on the motives of the peacemakers and on the effectiveness of the arrangements made in Vienna and Paris.

▶ Make a list of the representatives of the major states to give some substance to your answers.

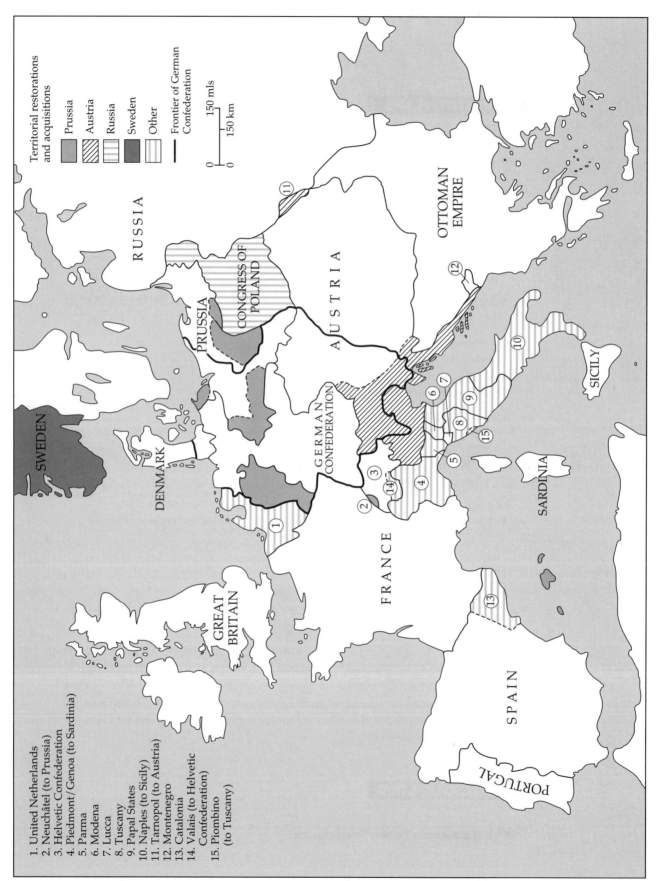

Territorial restorations and acquisitions

Prussia
Austria
Russia
Sweden
Other

Frontier of German Confederation

150 mls
150 km

RUSSIA

CONGRESS OF POLAND

PRUSSIA

SWEDEN

DENMARK

AUSTRIA

OTTOMAN EMPIRE

GERMAN CONFEDERATION

GREAT BRITAIN

FRANCE

SPAIN

PORTUGAL

SARDINIA

SICILY

1. United Netherlands
2. Neuchâtel (to Prussia)
3. Helvetic Confederation
4. Piedmont/Genoa (to Sardinia)
5. Parma
6. Modena
7. Lucca
8. Tuscany
9. Papal States
10. Naples (to Sicily)
11. Tarnopol (to Austria)
12. Montenegro
13. Catalonia
14. Valais (to Helvetic Confederation)
15. Piombino (to Tuscany)

Map 1: Europe after The Vienna Peace Settlement of 1815   *Source:* Briggs and Clavin, *Modern Europe 1789–1989*, Longman, 1997

▶ Use Map 1, showing the political boundaries, to revise the changes made.
▶ List the motives of the peacemakers (remember to include restoring the pre-war situation, preventing a future war, creating a balance of power, keeping a curb on France).
▶ Revise the creation of the Holy Alliance and the Quadruple Alliance.
▶ Decide what you need to revise in order to be able to assess how effective the peace arrangements were (Congress system, peace for forty years).

1815–70 France

This topic falls into clearly defined periods but to maximize your revision effort you probably need to revise the internal history of France across the full period. You will then be very unfortunate if you do not get at least one examination question as your reward.

1815–30 Bourbon Restoration

▶ Revise this period in terms of how successful the restoration of the monarchy was under Louis XVIII (1815–24), the initial problems he faced and how effectively France was governed.
▶ Then revise the increasingly reactionary rule of Charles X and the reasons for the overthrow of the monarchy in the 1830 Revolution.
▶ Be ready for a question that expects an assessment of the period as a whole.

1830–48 Louis-Philippe

▶ Revise the reign as a whole, listing problems which arose and why the government proved less and less competent in dealing with these; a weak foreign policy is part of the story.
▶ The most common examination questions relate to why the monarchy was overthrown in 1848.

1848–52 Second French Republic

▶ Revise the events of 1848 in France in relation also to the end of Louis-Philippe and for possible use in a Europe-wide essay on the 1848 revolutions.
▶ Any other questions are likely to relate to the failure of the republic and the reasons for Louis Napoleon's seizure of power. Remind yourself of his own and his family background.

1852–70 Napoleon III and the Second Empire

▶ Napoleon III's rule had to live up to his family legend. List the things his supporters might expect from him.
▶ Understand the autocratic nature of his rule in the 1850s and why he tried to introduce a more liberal regime in the 1860s.
▶ List his reforms and the changes that occurred in France in this period.
▶ Use these to construct an overall assessment of what the empire did for France prior to the disasters of 1870.
▶ Revise the foreign policy because this is an essential, if increasingly unsuccessful, part of the record.
▶ Revise in detail what happened in 1870 and how far Napoleon was responsible (this will, for some candidates, also be the beginning of post-1870 study of the Third French Republic).

1815–48 Repressive policies of Metternich

Metternich's long career embraced several key episodes in European history from 1815 to 1848:

▶ He was the Austrian representative at the 1814–15 Peace Settlement where he played a major part in drawing up the final terms.

▶ He was fully involved in the work of the Congress system, particularly in relation to the suppression of popular revolts in the Italian states where he was always a staunch supporter of the small autocratic Italian states.

▶ Much of his time was committed to maintaining the ramshackle Austrian Empire, employing repressive policies to stamp out nationalist outbreaks.

▶ He also devoted much energy to preventing liberal and nationalist developments in the 300-plus states of the German Confederation set up in 1815, notably with the 1819 Carlsbad Decrees.

▶ In 1848 much of his work was temporarily swept away by the revolts across Europe and his own political career ended at that point.

You will need to revise all of these interlinked topics in order to be ready to answer a question on Metternich. The period from the end of the Congress system to 1848 is often briefly studied, outside French history at least, simply as an introduction to later more clear-cut topics like the 1848 revolutions, Italian unification and German unification. Its complexity seems to make it a minority interest in terms of actually answering examination questions.

1848 Revolutions across Europe

Map 2 shows the centre of revolutions in Europe in 1848

Map 2: Centres of revolution in Europe 1848
Source: Briggs and Clavin, *Modern Europe 1789–1989*, Longman, 1997

▶ Questions on the causes of the revolutions across Europe require knowledge of events in the various countries prior to 1848. You also need to understand the terms liberalism and nationalism and be able to explain their significance in nineteenth-century Europe.

▶ Make a list of the countries where unrest occurred and the causes, events and consequences in each case, starting with France (use the map of Europe in 1815 to carry out a survey).

▶ The outcome of the revolts was usually disappointing for those who took part and almost everywhere (outside France) the old authoritarian order was restored.

▶ You will need detailed information on events in the Austrian Empire, the German Confederation and the Italian states.

Be able to explain why, in each case, the revolutions failed. This revision will have a double benefit when you move on to revise Italian and German unification.

1848–70 Unification of Italy

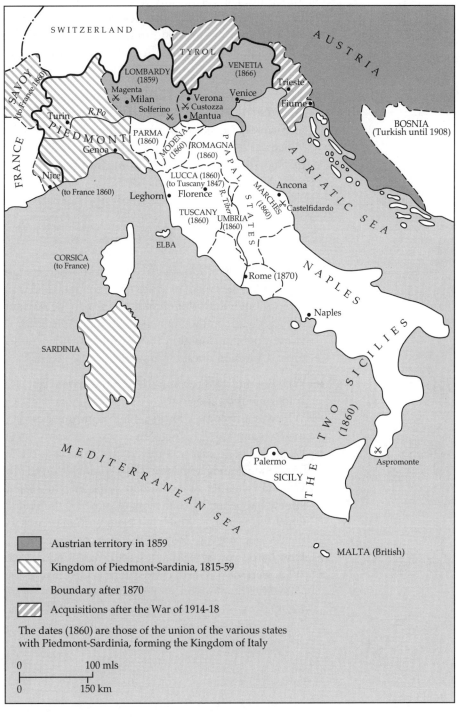

Map 3: Italian Unification 1859–70

Source: Briggs and Clavin, *Modern Europe 1789–1989*, Longman, 1997

The map of Europe and your study of 1848 will provide the necessary background. Most questions on this very popular examination topic start after 1848 and it is then a mistake to spend examination time giving background information for its own sake. Try to get directly to the terms of the question. Common questions include:

▶ Comparing the importance of Mazzini, Cavour and Garibaldi in the unification.
▶ Examining the role of one or more of these men in bringing about unification (Mazzini is usually the least well known).
▶ Cavour's motives: did he wish to expand Piedmont rather than unite Italy?
▶ How important was the role of Piedmont in bringing about unification?
▶ The role of foreign intervention both in promoting and in attempting to block unification. In this the roles of Austria, France, Britain and Prussia are all important. Did the actions of foreign powers do more to unite the country than the activities of Italian nationals? (see student answer pp. 86–7.)
▶ In what ways and to what extent did the way in which unification occurred affect later Italian history (often through to 1914)? (This type of question is not all that common.)

This topic seems to lend itself to quotation questions which candidates are then invited to discuss. Remember that quotation questions often exaggerate in order to encourage criticism of what is offered, so look for alternative explanations. Whatever the type of question, do remember that the topic is often taken right through to the absorption of Rome into Italy in 1870; do not end your revision with the death of Cavour in 1861.

1848–70 Unification of Germany

The 1815 map of Europe (p. 42) and knowledge of the arrangements made in 1815 for the German states are essential background to understanding this topic, though the detail should not usually be recounted at length in essays on unification. A simple time-chart on the events leading from the 1848 revolutions to eventual unification in 1871 would provide a useful structure for revision of this topic. Common questions include

▶ Why did the 1848 revolutions in the German states fail to make any headway in achieving unification?
▶ Why was it necessary for Prussia to confront Austria before it could take the lead in Germany?
▶ Explain why Prussia was able to oust Austria as the leading German state (this involves including some pre-1848 comment on the role of the Zollverein).
▶ Examine whether Bismarck had a master-plan to achieve unification or whether it largely happened by chance or, at most, by the skilful seizing of opportunities which came along. (Much has been written on this topic and it would pay, even at the revision stage, to look up the ideas of more than one historian on this.)
▶ How far do you agree that it was Bismarck (alone) who united Germany?
▶ What were the political consequences for Europe of German unification? (However, note that this topic in practice opens up all of European history to 1914; if you propose mainly to answer pre-1870 topics then you are unlikely to want to study the detail of the very different later period.)

1855–71 Reforms of Alexander II in Russia

The internal history of Russia across the nineteenth century is a sensibly self-contained topic for revision purposes, but the reigns of Alexander I and Nicholas I, from 1801 to 1855, are not nearly as common examination topics as the reign of Alexander II from 1855 to 1881. Nor do the standard textbooks provide information at much depth on the earlier reigns. Note:

▶ This topic goes on beyond 1870, though most important matters occurred before that date.
▶ Russian foreign policy, including the Crimean War (1854–56), is probably best treated as an essential part of any study of the Eastern Question, though Russia's importance in assisting autocratic states before and during the 1848 Revolutions is also worth noting.

Alexander II had to deal with

▶ the many inefficiencies in the administration and economy of the Russian state
▶ the catastrophic defeat in the Crimean War.

How these issues interlinked is a good revision starting-point from which you can construct an argument as to why Alexander realized that reforms were essential. Common examination questions include:

▶ Why did Alexander embark on a programme of reforms?
▶ The 1861 emancipation of the serfs as a separate topic (which needs studying over a long period, perhaps even through to the early twentieth century, so that the success of the emancipation and its effects on Russia can be commented on).
▶ How effective his reforms were in modernizing Russia (the serf emancipation, local government and army reforms were particularly important).
▶ Why did Alexander in his later years return to a policy of repression?
▶ What, overall, was the effect of his reign on Russian history? Was it a new starting-point after the Crimean War disasters or did the old Russian weaknesses and stagnation continue?

1815–70 The Eastern Question

This arose largely from the declining power of the Ottoman (Turkish) Empire which continued right across the nineteenth century. Russia wished to expand westwards at the expense of the Turks and this aroused the suspicion and the opposition of the Austrian Empire and Britain (Russian access to the Mediterranean) in particular. A series of international crises resulted and these are probably most economically revised as a unit through from 1815 to 1914. At each crisis you will have to remember that the international context was changing, with the 1870 unification of Germany a major turning-point. Revision issues for the Eastern Question are continued in the topic outline on European history 1870–1914 (see pp. 58–62), where the topic becomes an important part of any explanation of the outbreak of the First World War.

First look again at the map of Europe in 1815, then revise the following topics, all of which arise from the Eastern Question:

▶ 1820s Greek independence
▶ 1830s Mehemet Ali
▶ 1854–56 Crimean War, including both the causes of the war and the long-term results.

Useful information

Map

The political map of Europe after the 1815 Peace Settlement (p. 42) is an essential starting-point for political history through to at least 1870. Study it carefully.

Important terms

Use your textbook to familiarize yourself with the following so that you can use them confidently in your own writing: absolute monarchy, authoritarian, autocracy, balance of power, imperialism, liberalism, nationalism, socialism.

Important figures

Be ready to assess the careers of the following: Metternich, Louis XVIII, Charles X, Louis-Philippe, Napoleon III, Mazzini, Cavour, Garibaldi, Bismarck, Alexander II.

Some key dates in European history

▶ 1815 Vienna Peace Settlement
▶ 1830 end of restored French Bourbon monarchy
▶ 1848 revolutions throughout Europe
▶ 1852 Napoleon III became French Emperor
▶ 1854–56 Crimean War
▶ 1859–60 key moves towards Italian unification
▶ 1866 Prussian defeat of Austria
▶ 1870 Prussian defeat of France led to unification of Germany.

REVISION ACTIVITY

France 1815–70

(a) Draw up a simple time-chart of French history in the period. Identify the different blocks of time on which questions are usually set and scan past papers to note which topics come up most frequently.
(b) Within each block of time note the major items of content you could use to answer the questions set in the past.
(c) Think through how you would answer a question explaining the causes and the consequences of the revolution of 1830.
(d) Write a rough opening paragraph to answer the question 'Why did the Second French Republic (1848–52) collapse so quickly?'
(e) Make an essay plan (ideas rather than a list of content, though you can add that if you want) to answer the question 'How far do you agree that even before 1870 Napoleon III's foreign policy had done little or nothing to promote French national interests?'

Other revision ideas

Vienna Peace Settlement

Use the map of Europe in 1815 to help work out what were the chief features of the Vienna Peace Settlement. Cross-refer to past exam papers on the topic to see which are the likeliest questions to come up. You could then list the major powers represented at the settlement, with the names of their leading representative, and alongside each entry note in what ways their interests were 'looked after' in the agreed terms. Whose interests were ignored? Why did the Vienna statesmen either ignore or repress the ideas of liberalism and nationalism which had emerged from the French Revolution? (This could lead you on to revise the 1848 revolutions.)

Eastern Question

If you are intending to study the Eastern Question through from 1870 to 1914 then consider revising it in the period up to 1870 and check past papers for question frequency. Greek independence, Mehemet Ali and the Crimean War are the central topics in this period.

Alexander II

Russian domestic history is a self-contained topic so consider widening your range of question choices by revising the career of the 'reforming Tsar' Alexander II and preparing an assessment of the effect of his work on Russia. If your examination period continues to 1914, it would be economical on effort also to revise at least the reign of the last Tsar, Nicholas II. The specialized topic on the emancipation of the serfs deserves a second look to remind yourself of Russia's social and economic weaknesses at the time of the Crimean War. However, the effects also need to be revised through to the early-twentieth-century and the work of Stolypin.

European history 1870–1914

Now turn to the topic outline on European history 1870–1914 and think how you can generally maximize your efforts by extending early- and mid-nineteenth-century topics into the period to 1914. French history under the Third Republic (to 1914) and German domestic history and foreign policy under Bismarck (to 1890) are obvious examples.

PRACTICE QUESTIONS

Essay questions

Question 1

How far do you agree that foreigners were more important than Italians in bringing about the unification of Italy?

Question 2

To what extent was the unification of Germany a result of planning and to what extent a matter of chance and opportunism?

European history 1870–1914

✓ REVISION TIPS

In this period examiners seem to be particularly interested in international issues: these centre around two themes:

- ▶ 1870–1914 The Eastern Question
- ▶ Origins of the First World War
  - – background
  - – events of 1914
  - – debate on who was responsible

The second theme, which is the one on which questions are most commonly set, arises from the first and so, unless past papers contradict the advice, there is a lot to be said for revising both topics in sequence.

- ▶ Start with the political map of Europe showing just national boundaries pre-1914.
- ▶ As you revise, construct a simple time-chart of major international issues of the period.
- ▶ Think through a list of the possible issues that might cause trouble between the major powers in Eastern Europe (you probably do not even need to write them down at this stage).
- ▶ What, in the same period, were the issues between France and Germany?
- ▶ This is often described as a period of European imperialism; check past papers to see if imperial rivalry, mainly in Africa, is worth revising as an examination topic. If not, or if it doesn't interest you, at least know enough to be able to write a paragraph on how imperial rivalry affected relations between European powers, especially Britain and France, Britain and Germany, and Germany and France. A political map of pre-1914 Africa would help at this stage.
- ▶ How Europe, after 1890, became divided into two armed camps and how, in 1914, this led to the catastrophic First World War, is by far the single most important issue of the period.

Domestic issues

It also seems that examiners have favourite topics relating to the internal history of the powers, though the precise thrust of the questions is here often less easy to predict. Most of the domestic history questions in this period come from the following topics:

- ▶ 1871–90 Germany under Bismarck
- ▶ 1870–1914 Third French Republic
- ▶ 1894–1917 Russia under Nicholas II
- ▶ 1867–1918 Austro-Hungarian Empire

The internal history of the multinational Austro-Hungarian Empire is important not so much as a source of domestic history questions but because it helps to explain so much of the growing international crisis – look again at the map of pre-1914 Europe! Please note that, because so much of the international history of the period is set within the framework originated by Bismarck, this and the other two domestic history topics identified above have been placed first among the topic outlines which follow.

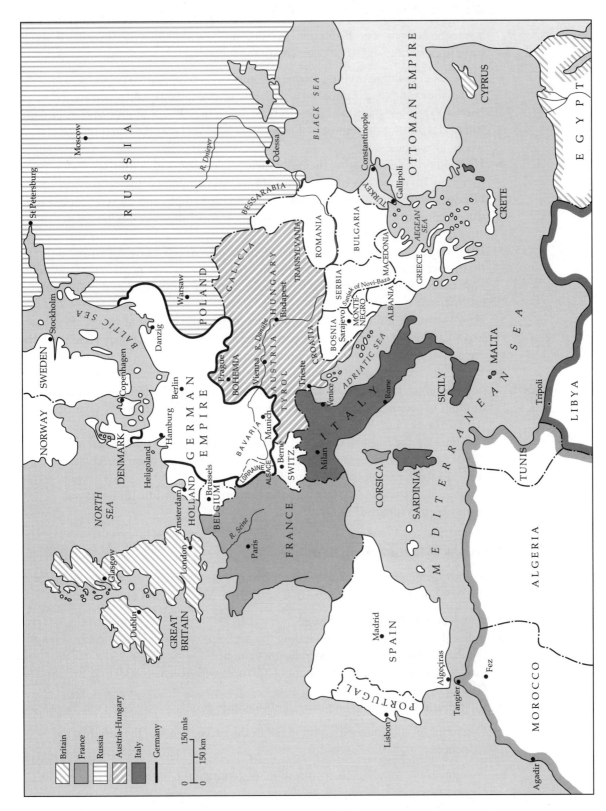

Map 4: Europe 1914   *Source:* Briggs and Clavin, *Modern Europe 1789–1989*, Longman, 1997

TOPIC OUTLINE

1871–90 Germany under Bismarck

The central focus is on Bismarck's policies and assessing his achievements. The most important issues to be covered are the following:

▶ His work in building up the German Empire and creating a German identity (using, for example, the imperial army, the railway, the post and a common currency) but one based as far as possible on his own Prussian state and its Junker ruling class. An understanding of how the empire was governed as a federal state would be a useful start.

▶ His methods of dominating the parliament (Reichstag) and getting his own way there; his 1870s wooing of the National Liberals helped to achieve this.

▶ His quarrel with the Catholic Church (the Kulturkampf), the causes, events and the compromise which ended the dispute; how much Bismarck achieved in this episode is an important issue.

▶ His dispute with the socialists (Social Democrats), his repressive measures and their survival. Again an assessment of his success and failure is needed and should include knowledge of the social welfare measures he introduced and his reasons for this.

▶ How Germany, unified in 1871 and undergoing rapid industrialization after that, was soon potentially the greatest of the European continental powers and how this created an entirely new international situation.

▶ Bismarck's foreign policy, based on his anxiety to avoid German involvement in war, required close relations with Austria while keeping the friendship of Russia, in order to prevent France finding an East European ally. His policy is worth reading up because it has double value in also laying a basis for answering questions on the Eastern Question. His aims and his success in foreign affairs to 1890 contrast with German policy after 1890; this in turn helps to explain the drift to a major European War in 1914.

▶ How Bismarck worked closely with the Emperor William I to 1888 but was dismissed by William II in 1890.

1870–1914 Third French Republic

Many examination questions ask for a broad assessment of the progress made by the republic from the defeat of 1870 until 1914. You need information on

▶ population and economic change
▶ political instability at home including the problems with the Catholic Church and the development of a strong socialist movement
▶ growth of empire and development of alliances with Russia (1893) and Britain (1904)
▶ the cultural flowering in late-nineteenth-century France.

Questions on specific topics tend to fall in the earlier years of the republic's existence:

▶ creation of the republic, its constitution, negotiating the humiliating peace with Germany
▶ Paris Commune 1870 and its defeat
▶ the royalist threat to 1875 and why it came to nothing
▶ Boulanger affair of the late 1880s
▶ Panama Scandal 1889
▶ Dreyfus affair 1894–1906.

Many candidates can tell the story of each of these interesting episodes but you need to be able to go on to relate them to the issue of the strengths and weaknesses, and indeed the survival, of the republic. Remember that the Third Republic survived to 1940 (or arguably 1946) though very few questions take its history beyond 1914.

1894-1917 Russia under Nicholas II

It is certainly worth revising this topic through to the end of Tsardom in February 1917. The weakness of the monarchy and the problems it faced will provide a clear revision theme with one great issue in what would have happened if war had not come in 1914. Would political and economic changes have transformed Russia or was the system so fossilized that it was doomed? This is unanswerable but it provides a useful insight into how to organize Russian pre-1914 history for revision purposes. Topics to revise include:

- ► role of Tsar Nicholas II (and the Tsarina Alexandra together with Rasputin)
- ► Russo-Japanese War 1904-05
- ► causes, events and results of the 1905 Revolution
- ► reforms of Witte, including an assessment of their effects
- ► work of Stolypin and its effects, including the parliamentary system (the Dumas)
- ► pre-1914 growth of opposition to Tsardom
- ► why Russia went to war in 1914 and how this helped bring about the end of Tsardom.

These topics need to be set in an overall assessment of why Tsardom fell.

1867-1918 Austro-Hungarian Empire

The best starting-point, yet again, is a map to remind yourself of the empire's strategic position in central Europe linking with almost all the important international issues of the period.

- ► In the 1860s it was pushed out of Italy and defeated by Prussia.
- ► In 1867 the imperial government was reorganized as a joint Austro-Hungarian Empire (the Ausgleich or compromise).

The aspirations of the other nationalities of the empire, particularly the Czechs and the Slav nationalities like the Serbs and the Croats, were a persistent problem to the empire. Their national aspirations threatened its very existence and were linked to pressing foreign issues on the empire's southern border. In the more important field of foreign affairs the following themes stand out:

- ► deteriorating relations with expanding Slav Serbia to the south
- ► rivalry with Russia for dominance in the Balkans as the Ottoman Empire crumbled away
- ► dependence on the long-lasting alliance with Germany.

These themes all came to a head in the crisis of 1914 in which Austria-Hungary played a central role; understand the state's history for this reason, if no other.

1870-1914 The Eastern Question

This topic needs to be studied, at least briefly, across the century from 1815, so first consult the topic outline on European history 1815-70 (pp. 41-8).

The decline of the Ottoman Empire continued after 1870 and the ambitions of both Russia and Austria-Hungary to replace it as the leading Balkan power continued to grow. The new factor in the region was the growing ambition of the separate Balkan nations. Most important of these was Serbia whose desire to embrace all Slavs living in the region threatened the integrity of the multiracial Austro-Hungarian Empire. Key episodes to revise are:

- ► 1878 Congress of Berlin; this had importance across Europe and often stands as an examination question in its own right. Both the reasons for Bismarck to call it and the success or otherwise of the arrangements made at the Congress need to be revised.
- ► 1908 Austrian annexation of Bosnia and why it provoked an international crisis.
- ► 1912–13 the two Balkan Wars and how their outcome made a future conflict more likely.

Little of the Eastern Question will make sense unless the interests in the region of both Austria-Hungary and Russia are understood. Russia's links with Serbia are then central to explanations of why war broke out in 1914.

Origins of the First World War (background)

There is a lot of background to grasp. Unfortunately examination time is strictly limited. You may have to study a great deal of detail but you will need to get to the essential issues quickly; in doing this above all remember to stay close to the precise terms of the question. Do not be trapped into telling the story of international relations in Europe in the decades before 1914. You need to be able to explain how the following contributed to a tense international situation by 1914:

- ► Franco-German rivalry
- ► Austro-Russian rivalry in the Balkans (which follows on from the Eastern Question)
- ► Serbian nationalism in the Balkans
- ► emergence of the two rival European alliance systems after 1890 and especially the close ties between Germany and Austria
- ► how imperial rivalries and the arms race increased international tension
- ► how Britain became drawn into the Franco-Russian alliance system
- ► how international crises prior to 1914 can be seen as making war more likely (the most important of these crises were the Bosnian Crisis 1908 and the Balkan Wars 1912–13).

All this can become very complicated and you must look up past questions to see what kinds of questions the examiners tend to ask. This will give you the best clue as to how much detail you will have time to use in an examination question.

Origins of the First World War (events of 1914)

Inevitably the immediate events of June–July 1914 make sense only in the context of the background of the previous decade at least. In a vast topic like the origins of the First World War, examiners have to devise questions which restrict the range of the topic. They quite often attempt to focus on the events of 1914. You will still have to explain the importance of these by reference to earlier years but it is important that you show a full grasp of the 1914 sequence, in particular:

- ► be able to explain how the assassination in Bosnia of the heir to the Austrian throne came immediately to involve Serbia and quite quickly Russia
- ► how Germany almost automatically backed Austria
- ► why this drew in France (look up the Schlieffen Plan)
- ► how Britain was, a little reluctantly, drawn in via the German attack through Belgium
- ► how the drift to war seemed to take on an unstoppable momentum of its own
- ► how quickly it all happened.

In the spring of 1914 Europe seemed to be more stable than for years but by the end of July it was engulfed in a war of unimaginable horror which was to alter the political map of the continent almost beyond recognition. The challenge for you is to be able to explain why this happened and to do this effectively within the confines of an examination essay.

Origins of the First World War (debate on who was responsible)

Much has been written on this by historians and it has become one of the classic historical debates between different groups of historians. It is difficult enough for examination candidates to analyse the origins of the war without getting involved in the usually sterile debate about which historian claimed what and who refuted this. Unless your examination board likes such questions (which are often described as historiographical questions) then it might well be wise to settle for and polish your own views on the origins of the war. It is perhaps still worth noting the following:

▶ After the war, at the Versailles Peace Settlement, the Allies forced Germany to acknowledge its 'guilt' for starting the war and, on this basis, proceeded to punish Germany.

▶ This provoked great resentment in Germany and even non-German historians came to argue that the causes of the war were complex and no one nation could be held responsible for starting it.

▶ More recently a German historian, Fritz Fischer, argued to the contrary that German actions had contributed crucially to the outbreak of war. The full backing given to Austria reflected the warlike mood among German politicians who saw a successful war as a means of breaking the Allied encirclement. Increasingly historians in the 1990s acknowledged that there was much in this argument and so the guilt issue seemed to come full circle.

In outline papers this may be all the historical interpretation you need to back up your own ideas. In any case the most important point to make is that no one in 1914 envisaged a war on the scale that actually occurred. In origin it was just another little Balkan War, which Austria and Germany were prepared to risk. The alliance system then sucked in the other powers into what, even then, they thought would be a short war.

Useful information

Map
The pre-1914 political map of Europe (p. 51) is essential to understanding the international rivalries.

Important terms
Be able to understand and to use the following: arms race, balance of power, defensive alliance, entente, imperialism, jingoism, militarism, nationalism, social Darwinism.

Important figures
Be ready to assess the careers of the following: Bismarck, Kaiser William II, Tsar Nicholas II, Witte, Stolypin.

★ REVISION ACTIVITY

The Eastern Question
Study a political map of Eastern Europe after 1870 and also remind yourself of the major features of the Eastern Question in the Topic Outline on European history 1815–70 (p. 47).

(a) Draw up a list of the main issues related to the Congress of Berlin in sufficient detail for it to become a plan for an essay answer.

(b) Work round the map of Eastern Europe and rehearse to yourself the interests and the role in the Eastern Question of at least the Ottoman (Turkish) Empire, Austria-Hungary, Russia and Serbia. Think why, from time to time, Germany, France and Britain found themselves involved in crises there.

(c) Rehearse, either in your head or at paragraph length on paper, how you would argue that the Bosnian Crisis 1908 and the Balkan Wars 1912–13 made a general war over the Balkans more likely. Know enough to be able to expand your paragraph with some factual backing.

Other revision ideas

Domestic history

First decide how much attention you intend to give to the internal history of

▶ Bismarck's Germany, which is worth preparing as a second preference question to Germany's role in international affairs.

▶ The Third French Republic to 1914; some outline examination papers contain several questions on nineteenth-century France, so this may well be a sensible addition (of course in the light of past papers) to French topics earlier in the century.

▶ Tsarist Russia, which you should consider taking through to the end of Tsardom in 1917.

Then follow up the revision proposals on these subjects in the topic outlines above, which should prove fairly straightforward if linked to specific questions from past papers.

PRACTICE QUESTIONS

Essay questions

Question 1

How far do you agree that there is 'much to be said for the view that Germany brought about the First World War'?

Question 2

To what extent was the existence of the system of alliances responsible for the outbreak of a general European war in 1914?

8 *European history 1914–45*

You will need to decide how much attention you intend to give to the First World War. In outline papers, questions appear mainly on its military aspects on the Western Front but their precise focus can be a bit of a lottery. Military history is for those who are really interested. Option paper syllabuses usually start at the end of the First World War and run through to 1939, though some are even more narrowly based and focus, for example, just on Nazi Germany, where the theme is taken through to 1945. Do look at recent past examination papers.

European history in the period 1919 to 1939 is the single most popular topic studied at A-level. The most common topics on which examiners ask questions relate to the three important dictatorships of the period (in Soviet Union, Italy and Germany) and to the build-up, in the 1930s, to the Second World War, including:

► Results of the First World War and the Versailles Peace Settlement
► 1917–41 Soviet Union under Lenin and Stalin
► Mussolini and fascism in Italy
► Weimar Republic and the rise of Hitler to 1933
► Nazi Germany from 1933 (either to 1939 or to 1945)
► Origins of the Second World War
  – background
  – debate
► 1936–39 Spanish Civil War
► 1939–45 Second World War

The amount of time you spend on revising any one of these topics should be strictly regulated by the balance of questions in past papers set by your examination board:

► Start by reminding yourself of what the map of Europe (p. 58) looked like after the peacemakers at Versailles had redrawn it.
► Note the effects of the First World War on the Soviet Union and on Germany both by using the map and from your notes.
► Be ready to comment on the disintegration of the Austro-Hungarian Empire and its replacement by a number of small nation-states.
► Return to the map of Europe when you come to revise the events of the 1930s leading up to the outbreak of the Second World War.
► Start to revise the 1930s by constructing a time-chart as a reminder of the sequence of crises from 1931 to 1939.

Examination questions are rarely set on French domestic history and those set on the smaller European nations, dictatorships in Hungary or Poland for example, occur so infrequently that they are of doubtful value as revision tasks. The outstanding exception is Spain and the Spanish Civil War 1936–39, on which questions often appear. If you are studying the 1930s in British history, knowledge of events in Europe in the 1930s will give an excellent basis for questions on British foreign policy leading up to the Second World War.

Map 5: Europe after the Paris Peace Conference
Source: Briggs and Clavin, *Modern Europe 1789–1989*, Longman, 1997

TOPIC OUTLINE

Results of the First World War and the Versailles Peace Settlement

▶ Study the map of the arrangements made at the Paris Peace Conference in 1919.
▶ Set this alongside the political map of Europe in 1914 (see Topic Outline on European history 1870–1914, p. 52).
▶ List the main territorial consequences of the war.
▶ Revise from a textbook the results of the war for Russia (the Soviet Union), Austria-Hungary and the nation-states which succeeded it and for Germany.

The outcome of the war greatly affected the internal history of the European states and also set the scene for the events which led once more to war in 1939. The First World War created the framework for European history between the wars.

1917–41 Soviet Union under Lenin and Stalin

Start your revision with the events of the October Revolution 1917, which brought the Bolsheviks to power. The causes of the revolution will take you back into earlier Russian history and are worth revising only if your outline paper covers the earlier period back to before 1914. The most important examination issues of the Lenin period (1917–24) are:

► the methods by which the communists established and defended the Soviet state from internal enemies, including the establishment of War Communism
► civil war against the White armies
► political and economic organization of the state
► change of direction with the introduction of the New Economic Policy
► assessing the contribution of Lenin to the Soviet Union
► assessing the career of Trotsky both in 1917 and after
► power struggle after Lenin's death
► Soviet relations with other states and the failure of the attempt to export revolution.

The most common questions involve an assessment of Lenin's role. In answer you may well have to describe what Lenin did but do also include lots of comments on why his various actions were important. The best answers recognize that he did not establish the Soviet Union on his own and acknowledge, for example, the importance of Trotsky's work.

Questions on the Soviet Union under Stalin include the following:

► His outwitting rivals in the 1920s to gain total power in the state.
► The creation of a command economy controlled by the state.
► His industrial and agrarian policies in the 1930s and an assessment of what was achieved economically in these years. Weaker essays are often thin on evidence and a few statistics and specific examples can strengthen essays significantly.
► The purges of the 1930s, which need to be separated into the destruction of the kulaks to 1934 and the political purges of the late 1930s. What, if any, were the reasons for the purges and what were the consequences for the Soviet state?
► Soviet foreign policy in the 1930s and especially the August 1939 Nazi-Soviet Pact and its international consequences.

The logical finishing-point is 1941, with the German invasion of the Soviet Union. Essay questions on Stalin rarely require answers to continue across the war years and on to his death in 1953.

Mussolini and fascism in Italy

This topic seems to interest examiners more than Italy's importance in general European history justifies; this is clearly because Mussolini created the first fascist dictatorship, during the ten years before Hitler came to power in Germany. The new right-wing totalitarian state attracted much contemporary comment and it retains its hold in present-day history papers. Common topics to revise include

► The reasons why Mussolini became Prime Minister in 1922, which involves explaining the weaknesses of the democratic Italian state and the disillusionment of the Italian people in the post-war period. Some pre-war history may be useful but do make it directly relevant to the question set. This topic is a danger area for those tempted to offer long descriptive accounts of the background.
► The attraction of the fascist movement and fascist ideas to many Italians (which Italians?).
► How Mussolini, from 1922 to 1928–29, secured dictatorial power including an explanation of the weaknesses of his opponents.
► The organization of the fascist state (the ideas of the Corporate State).
► An assessment of what Mussolini did for Italy domestically.
► Mussolini's foreign policy and how it changed after 1934. Draw up a time-chart and take the analysis through to 1940 when Italy joined the Second World War. The war against Ethiopia is a major topic in the international history of the 1930s.

Any assessment of Mussolini's contribution to Italian history should extend to 1943, when with defeat in war looming he was overthrown, or even to his death in 1945.

Weimar Republic and the rise of Hitler to 1933

The republic was born in the defeat of war. Common examination topics include

▶ How Weimar survived the crises of the early years (to 1923). Some candidates lack adequate knowledge to do this well and you should avoid this trap. Revise the weaknesses and the crises (Spartacists, Kapp Putsch and Hitler's Munich Putsch) and be able to explain why Weimar survived them. Make a list of groups opposing the regime and also a list of the factors which enabled Weimar to survive.

▶ An assessment of Stresemann's contribution to Weimar. He was briefly in charge of the economy and appointed Schacht to reform the currency (often forgotten by weaker candidates) but then was mainly involved in foreign policy.

▶ The stability and prosperity in the years from 1924, the depth of which are now often queried.

▶ The early years of the Nazi movement, its ideas and its limited appeal pre-1929.

▶ How Hitler came to power between 1929 and 1933. This is the most common topic on examination papers and should be revised in detail including knowledge of Nazi tactics (legal or not?), of how economic problems helped the Nazis electorally (be able to quote election figures) and how political intrigues among other right-wing leaders led to his becoming Chancellor.

Nazi Germany from 1933

The amount of detail you will need to master will depend on whether you are studying this topic as part of an outline paper or as part of the syllabus of a narrowly focused option paper. Your best guide will come from close study of the questions on immediate past papers. Common examination questions include

▶ How in 1933–34 did the Nazis consolidate their power? (This can link to pre-1933 questions.)

▶ Assess the experience of the German people under Nazism up to 1939. Did they have reason to be satisfied with Nazi rule? (It is sensible in answers to this type of question to identify different groups of Germans and distinguish between them in terms of the question set.)

▶ Why was there so little opposition to the Nazis? (This involves knowing what opposition there was.)

▶ Nazi social and economic policies and the creation of a totalitarian state. (These can include educational and youth policies, employment and trade union matters, the use of propaganda, the repression of potential opponents and racial policies.)

If your period of study goes on to 1945 then it is very important that, under each of these headings, you are able to distinguish between the pre-war and the war periods. Under the pressure of total war, and soon looming defeat, much changed, usually for the worse, as with the intensification of the anti-Jewish policies into the horror of the Holocaust. This, in its European rather than just its German context, stands as the most important 'social' topic of the period to 1945.

Hitler's foreign policy is considered under the next topic heading.

Origins of the Second World War (background)

▶ Study again the map of Europe in 1919; note particularly the situation of Austria, Czechoslovakia and also Poland, dividing Germany in two.

▶ Construct a time-chart of the crises of the 1930s.

▶ Remember that in a history examination you will have to do more than describe what happened. Check past papers to see the problems that interest examiners.

▶ Hitler's actions provide the clearest route through most of the various crises but do not assume that he had some master-plan which inevitably and successfully unfolded.

▶ You need to be ready for a question which asks how far he had planned his foreign policy and how far he simply took advantage of opportunities as they arose. Remember he also made mistakes and miscalculated – his attack on Poland was based on a belief that Britain and France would yet again take no action. It was to prove a costly miscalculation for all of Europe.

▶ Another common question is to invite discussion of how far the Allied policy of appeasement encouraged Hitler and so made war more likely. (In British history papers a frequent recent question has been based on the contrary proposal that appeasement was a perfectly sensible policy for Britain to pursue.)

▶ The impotence of the League of Nations is often important in questions on why aggression was not checked; the Japanese aggression against China from 1931 and Italy's attack on Ethiopia in 1935 are the key episodes to discuss.

▶ The Soviet Union's poor relations with France and Britain, culminating in the Nazi–Soviet Pact of August 1939, is an important theme.

▶ Events from September 1938 to August 1939, from Munich to the German attack on Poland, require detailed study: questions are frequently asked on the events of this one year alone. You should be ready for a question on why peace was maintained in the one year but war broke out in the next.

Now read the next entry on the historical debate about the origins of the war.

Origins of the Second World War (debate)

This is one of the topics that have developed great controversy among historians and, in option papers especially, some examination boards set questions which invite analysis of or comment on this debate. If past papers have had such (historiographical) questions, you will need to decide how much attention to give to them. Historical essays are, however, complicated enough to write without having to deliver long lists of the names of historians and describe what the argument of each was. If in the examination you can avoid a historiographical approach, then all you need are one or two of the key points of the historians' debate to give some convincing depth to your own ideas on why the war occurred. The following are perhaps the most important points of the debate:

▶ Soon after 1945 Churchill wrote a history of the war in which he argued that Hitler had all along intended the domination of Europe by war and that the feebleness of Britain and France from 1933 to 1939 simply encouraged him. This view held sway for over 20 years.

▶ A J P Taylor in the 1960s provided a controversial counter-argument that, far from having a plan, Hitler was the supreme opportunist, taking advantage of chances as they came. He dismissed both *Mein Kampf* and the Hossbach memorandum (look both up) as evidence for the contrary view.

▶ Work up your own view of Hitler's strategy and then incorporate these different interpretations into this but, unless you really have to, avoid rote learning of the interpretations of a list of historians. Note that recent historical writing has seen more sense of purpose behind Hitler's foreign policy.

1936–39 Spanish Civil War

This is a usefully self-contained topic for revision purposes. Note:

▶ The causes of the war require revision but you should avoid telling the story of Spanish history over previous decades. This topic seems to encourage long descriptive accounts when in practice it requires as much analytical effort as any other topic.

▶ You will need enough information on the course of the war to explain why the fascists won, but during revision organize it logically for that purpose. There is no virtue in being able to give a year by year account of the war.

▶ The most common single question on the war requires discussion of how far the fascist victory was a result of foreign intervention.

1939–45 Second World War

Questions are sometimes asked on the military history of the war:

▶ Account for the German victories from 1940 to 1942 or the ultimate Allied victory.

▶ Examine the importance of sea warfare or airpower in deciding the outcome of the war.

These are useful questions if you have a particular interest in military matters but not otherwise. Other questions concern wartime diplomacy, particularly that associated with holding the alliance against Hitler together. The Second World War opened up a completely new era of European international history which is most commonly found in history examination papers stretching well into the second half of the twentieth century. Except for the internal affairs of Nazi Germany, the war period is not usually tacked on to the inter-war period. It is essential that you check past papers before getting deeply involved.

Useful information

Maps
You need the map of Europe in 1919 (p. 58) and also maps showing German expansion in the 1930s.

Important terms
Make sure that you understand and can use the following: appeasement, blitzkrieg, communism, fascism, Holocaust, liberalism, nationalism, Nazism, popular front, totalitarian, total war.

Important figures
Be ready to assess the careers and the importance of: Lenin, Stalin, Trotsky, Mussolini, Stresemann, Hitler, Franco, Chamberlain, Churchill.

REVISION ACTIVITY

Soviet Union

(a) Draw up a list of the main issues of the period from October 1917 to the death of Lenin in 1924. Which of these would you use to assess Lenin's importance in setting up the communist state?

(b) Prepare an essay plan to answer the question ' "Ruthless but necessary": examine this verdict on Stalin's purges in the 1930s.'

(c) Write the final paragraph of this essay.

(d) List the issues to refer to in an essay explaining the nature and scale of the economic changes in the Soviet Union in the 1930s.

Other revision ideas

Paris Peace Settlement
Study the political map of Europe in 1919 and work out what political problems were created by the Paris Peace Settlement and how these affected the course of events in the 1930s.

Spanish Civil War

Prepare essay plans for

▶ a question on why the Spanish Civil War occurred
▶ a question on explaining why the Nationalists won the war (be prepared in particular to assess the role of non-Spaniards in affecting the outcome of the war).

Second World War

Prepare your argument for why the Second World War occurred, including

▶ Hitler's role – master plan or opportunist?
▶ the responsibility of the Franco-British appeasement policy
▶ the role of the Soviet Union.

Work through the international events from 1933, but do not spend too long on the earlier material in the many questions limited to 1938–39. Avoid being too descriptive in answers that require argument and analysis.

PRACTICE QUESTIONS

Essay questions

Question 1

'By 1934 Hitler had established his total control of the German state and had done this by totally legal means.' Discuss.

Question 2

How far do you agree that fascist rule in Italy had, by 1939, brought substantial benefits to the country?

Note that, in the Part IV practice examination paper with suggested answers, there is a document question on the rise of Hitler (pp. 99–100).

part III
Answers and grading

Solutions
British domestic history 1815–68

SOLUTIONS TO REVISION ACTIVITY

The career of Lord Liverpool and the Liberal Tories to 1830

(a) Examples of repression include the suspension of Habeas Corpus, the Six (Gag) Acts, use of military, use of spies and agents provocateurs, backing Peterloo magistrates.

(b) Reforms include Huskisson's reductions in duties and removing barriers to trade, Peel's prison reforms and reduction in number of capital offences, repeal of the Combination Acts.

(c) The argument that 1822 was a great political turning-point should refer first to the new men who came into government and then set the instances of earlier repression against the post-1822 reforms.

(d) The idea of continuity across 1822 is now generally accepted. Your plan should include reference pre-1822 to non-repressive actions and defend Liverpool's need to maintain law and order in troubled times by firm government. Post-1822 you should point out the limited nature of the reforms (no political reforms) and suggest that the changes rest really on an improved economic climate. The main change in 1822 was in the personnel in top government jobs. Go through your notes and textbooks to try to develop an argument in favour of continuity for it will give you the most convincing answer to questions on this topic.

(e) On the Liberal Tories note that questions may go through to 1830 and, if this is the case, you must comment on the creation of the Metropolitan Police and Catholic Emancipation in addition to the Liverpool reforms. Define 'Liberal Tory' as someone prepared to grant reforms to improve social conditions in various ways but not willing to grant political or constitutional reforms.

ANSWERS TO PRACTICE QUESTIONS

Essay questions

Question 1 – Student answer
How far do you agree that it was disappointment at the terms of the 1832 Parliamentary Reform Act which led to the emergence of Chartism?

Certainly disappointment at the terms of the Act played some part in the emergence of Chartism but it is only one part of any explanation of its emergence as a mass political movement. Other factors such as anger at the harsh terms of the Whig Poor Law of 1834 and the growing pressure in the textile industry for some effective regulation of hours of work for adults also helped to create the Chartist movement. Chartism only really emerged as a mass movement when the political ideas of a few educated men like Lovett and Place began to attract wide support among the skilled working class of London and then wider support among the general working class in Birmingham and the textile towns of the north of England. This did not happen until at least 1838, six years after the passing of the Reform Act. Chartism's origins were complicated and not an immediate response to the disappointment of 1832.

That disappointment did however play a part. By leaving the workers outside the political system the Act provided fertile ground for those, like the handful of educated working-men who produced the Charter, seeking a further measure of political reform which would give a voice to members of the working class when they sought social or economic reforms. The terms of the Act with regard to the qualification to vote cut off almost all working-men from the franchise. The terms in county constituencies gave the vote only to those who owned land worth at least 40 shillings a year or who were tenants or leaseholders of much larger landholdings. There was no vote for the landless labourer. In the boroughs the £10 head of household qualification had slightly different effects in different parts of the country, depending on property values but it is fair to say that it operated, as those who drew up the Act intended, to leave the vote with men of substance from the middle class and cut out from the franchise almost all the working class. The other demands in the People's Charter show that the Act left the working class with other grievances, notably the absence of a secret ballot, but the restricted franchise was the central disappointment of the Chartists. Without it they had no political say and their other demands for reforms to purify parliament arose from this central fact. In the end this injustice would have led to some protest movement but the speed with which this emerged and its broad appeal came from other grievances which came to the fore in the later 1830s and for which the Whig government of the day must take some responsibility.

In the north of England a powerful working-class movement, led by Tory humanitarians like Fielden and Oastler, had grown up to try to gain some legal limitation of working hours for adults in the textile industries. This followed disappointment at the weaknesses of the 1833 Factory Act. As this movement lost its momentum in 1837 it was swept up into the emerging Chartist movement and in this region working grievances and class grievances against the wealthy manufacturers were one of the main reasons for men becoming Chartists. The other reason was hatred of the application of the 1834 Poor Law in the northern manufacturing towns with the introduction of the new workhouses into which the desperately poor would have to go in order to receive poor relief. A mass protest movement emerged, again often led by Tory humanitarians, and this too got swept up into the Chartist movement as it lost its own momentum in 1838 and 1839. In the north of England the political message of the Charter owed its appeal to pressing economic and social reasons rather than arising directly from political disappointment at the outcome in 1832.

In other parts of the country other motives were important. In East Anglia and in the South West of England the decline of traditional industries, especially handloom weaving of woollen cloth, made men political radicals. In Scotland poor living conditions in Glasgow and Edinburgh and sharp class differences everywhere were important reasons for the rise of Chartism.

Only in London can it be argued that political motives were of the greatest importance. This was because the class base of London Chartism was different from anywhere else. Educated working-class artisans, skilled workers and members of the lower middle class dominated in London. The mass of London's poor had no contact with Chartism. London provided the intellectual leadership of Chartism and it was here that the best case can be made out that disappointment at the timidity of the 1832 Reform Act was the main single cause of the emergence of Chartism. Even this is too simple, for political radicalism in London and elsewhere went back before 1832, in demands for political reform from the late eighteenth century strengthened by the messages of the French Revolution, and seen in the political demonstrations of the 1815 to 1822 period.

There were many reasons for the emergence of Chartism. The title of this essay greatly over-simplifies the reasons for its emergence and in particular neglects the role of social and economic grievances in promoting its advance. It also fails to do justice to the long tradition of political agitation going back long before 1832 and to the great local diversity within Chartism. It is therefore almost totally flawed as an explanation of the emergence of Chartism.

> **Examiner's comments** The great strength of this essay is its direct response to the question. It actually answers the question set from beginning to end and this would probably earn it an A grade despite its brevity and the thinness of its supporting information. The style and vocabulary are very sophisticated, the mark of a very able student, and no one should be put off by this. Few of us would write so effectively.
>
> The essay's main weakness is its failure to say anything about the way economic conditions, the recession of the late 1830s in many industries, contributed to the emergence of Chartism – this is a major gap in this student's analysis. More detail on how the 1832 Act disappointed the working class and the growing anger at the post-1832 Whig government, perhaps a mention of the way the Tolpuddle Martyrs trial inflamed public opinion and kept working-class radicalism alive in the 1830s, ready to be swept up into Chartism, would have given this brief essay more substance.

Question 2 – outline answer
'A great reforming ministry:' examine this comment on the Whig reforms of 1833 to 1841.

The easiest approach is to take each of the major reforms in turn. Do not get lost in describing the terms of the reforms, just give the main purpose of each and the problem to which it related. Then indicate its impact on the problem. For example the Municipal Reform Act closed down the old corrupt town corporations and, at a time of rapid urban growth, created a national pattern of town government responsible to ratepayer control via elections and capable of being given a range of urgent local jobs like public health provision. It was a very important reform. Then go on to the radical reorganizing of poor relief, the first effective Factory Act, the first education grant, the abolition of slavery and discuss the impact of each. You will need a clear general conclusion on the Whig record overall but it can be brief.

Document question

Question 3 – 1832 Reform Act

(a) (i) The Whig government.
   (ii) Any future Tory government which might come into power.
(b) *The Times* does not explicitly make its views on reform clear in this extract but there is no doubt where the paper stands. Reform is assumed to be 'a good thing' and it is seen to be in great danger. The entire extract is a cry for reform to be defended by preventing a Tory government. So it can certainly be inferred that the paper was resolutely and anxiously in favour of parliamentary reform.
(c) The purpose of *The Times* in this extract is to rally support for Lord Grey's attempt at reform and both the language and the tone are very effective in promoting this. The opening rhetorical question 'Well then what is to be done?' creates an idea of activity against the opponents of reform. The language strengthens this 'a determination not to endure for one moment' and 'a spirit must be manifested' and goes on 'throughout the UK' 'without losing another week'. All this language seeks to arouse the friends of reform, and those indifferent to it to act urgently against the threat of a Tory restoration and this emotional cry goes right on to the end of the extract with words like 'entreat' and the final cry for men who will vote 'through fire and water' for reform. The extract is an effective appeal to people's emotions rather than a reasoned argument about the merits of reform.
(d) From the extract you can certainly establish that *The Times* considered that outside pressure would be crucial in sustaining the momentum of reform. You should provide two or three brief quotations which show this to be the case. From your

own knowledge you need to widen the scope of your answer to mention particular examples of outside pressure, for example the riots in Bristol and Nottingham or the activities of the political pressure groups like Attwood's in Birmingham or the proposal to draw funds out of the banks, so ruining the country's finances, if reform was not conceded. The question asks 'how far do you agree' so it would be sensible to point out that only Parliament could pass reform and explain that some of the most critical moves came within Parliament; Grey threatening to swamp the Lords by having Whig Peers created is the most dramatic example. With 15 marks at stake this answer will need to be a substantial mini-essay, perhaps some two sides long.

Solutions
British domestic history 1868–1914

Disraeli

(a) For two reasons Disraeli's record as a social reformer was not impressive. Although several reforms were pushed through in the first year of his 1874–80 ministry the flow then dried up totally. Even with these early reforms his own input was limited with Cross, the Home Secretary, the more important figure. In imperial matters, on the other hand, although territorial gains were limited, his vision of empire and the activity in Africa and Afghanistan marked the beginning of a new expansion of the British Empire and British imperial influence.

(b) **Essay plan**

- ▶ Examine domestic record, argue Disraeli deserved limited credit for it – Cross's role, work of civil servants more important (give examples from legislation), many Acts only permissive, cite Artisans Dwellings Act and add how little impact it had on the housing problem. Use Merchant Shipping Act to illustrate legislation forced on government. Agree some things achieved but he doesn't deserve reputation for helping working class; there was no political reform. Explain how he lost interest in domestic policy for most of the ministry.
- ▶ Examine imperial record, stress importance of Cyprus and Suez Canal shares as extending British activity in and beyond the Mediterranean (explain how), agree practical achievements in Afghanistan and South Africa were limited and forced on him but in each case later ministries continued his policies. His imperial legacy was very important for he turned the Conservatives into the party of the empire and this affected later political life. The interest in southern Africa during his ministry was also linked to the great expansion of the empire there in the last decades of the nineteenth century.

Women

The essay plan on why women did not get the vote by 1914 should include the following points:

- ▶ The perceived role of women's place in Victorian society, their lack of other rights (property, family or career rights), include the indifference of many women, especially working-class women, to the issue.
- ▶ The difficulty of outsiders putting pressure on parliament for a major constitutional change, why Labour and the Liberals were not keen to help.
- ▶ The adverse effect of the shrill but increasingly ineffective suffragette campaign, making the Liberal government dig in rather than be seen as giving in to violence.

Question 1 – student answer
Why is Gladstone's 1868–74 ministry so often described as a 'great reforming ministry'?

There are three main reasons why Gladstone's ministry is seen as a great reforming ministry. First there was the great number of reform measures passed by the ministry. Second there was the seriousness of the problems that had to be remedied and third there was the long-term impact that some of the reforms had in the future.

The sheer number of reforming measures passed was impressive. They included Acts to deal with Irish grievances about religion and about the land which were passed early in the ministry as Gladstone sought 'to pacify Ireland'. Other Acts reorganized the army and the Civil Service, entry to the universities, the law about trade unions. Gladstone introduced the secret ballot in elections and he reorganized the court system for trials. He had a less successful Act to control the brewing and drinks industry but perhaps the most important Act was Forster's Education Act of 1870. This long list of reforms made this perhaps the most active reforming ministry of the nineteenth century. Both the seriousness of the problems and the effects of the reforms should now be considered.

Some of the reforms dealt with major problems. The poor state of the army had been shown by its incompetent organization during the Crimean War. Cardwell's army reforms changed the army administration totally, the purchase of commissions was abolished, infantry regiments were tied to counties, artillery regiments were increased, people signed on for the army for a shorter period of time. This 'new' army survived as the system of organization until 1914 and was a very important administrative reform. The other admin. reform was that of the Civil Service where in future entry was to be by exam and not by who you knew. This and other changes made the Civil Service more efficient in the long run which was important because the growing amount of social legislation had to be put into law and administered. Such laws could not have worked without a more efficient civil service.

The Irish Laws, the 1869 Disestablishment of the Irish Church and the 1870 Land Act also tried to deal with important problems of Irish grievances. The dislike of the Irish Catholics for the Church of England in Ireland went back centuries, they objected to its official position and to having to pay the tithe. Since the potato famine there had been serious economic problems in Ireland and very great bitterness against both the government and the great landowners. Gladstone's two Acts tried to remedy these problems. He deserves credit for being the first Prime Minister to try to tackle Irish problems by introducing reforms but the Acts did not end Irish unrest. A more radical Land Act came later but even then Irish grievances went on and became part of the movement for Home Rule. Gladstone did not in this ministry 'pacify Ireland'. Gladstone also introduced important laws regarding trade unions which were still not recognized by the law and so were not able even to protect their funds from dishonest treasurers. The Trade Union Act made unions legal and so ended this state of affairs and started a new stage in trade union history. Gladstone's government did not greatly increase union power to strike because a later Act made even peaceful picketing illegal.

The ministry introduced the most important education act of the nineteenth century in Forster's 1870 Education Act. This greatly extended the provision of elementary education to working-class children. Until 1870 schools had been provided by the Christian churches and there were many areas where there were no church schools or only poor church schools. For the first time the Act required elementary schools to be set up by newly formed school boards and paid for by local rates where there were no church schools. This 'filled the gaps' in the education system and was a massive extension of government interference in the role of the churches. Previously all the governments had done was to provide grants to the church schools but now it was requiring education to be available all over the country. This measure on its own makes Gladstone's ministry perhaps the greatest reforming ministry of the century.

Other reforms dealt with less important problems. The strong middle-class intolerance of alcohol and also of irresponsible behaviour among the working-class brought about Gladstone's Licensing Act which attempted to control the selling of alcoholic drinks. This was very unpopular and did the Liberals great harm politically. It did not enhance the government's reputation. The introduction of the Secret Ballot in elections on the other hand remedied a serious political abuse. After the 1867 Reform Act for the first time many working-men had the vote but were often afraid to use it as they wished because how they voted was known to their employers who could bully them into voting in a way the employer favoured. The Secret Ballot Act of 1872 ended this and made British politics more democratic and less corrupt by changing the way elections were conducted. The Judicature Act made the legal system much more efficient by reorganizing the High Courts of the country and set up an entirely new system of court appeals which survived into the second half of the twentieth century.

These reforms made Britain administratively more efficient and less corrupt. Some, as in Ireland and with the Licensing Act, did not solve the problems but others like in education, the army, the civil services, the courts and parliamentary elections changed dramatically the way things were and explain why Gladstone's ministry is generally seen as a great reforming one.

> *Examiner's comments* The essay has a strong opening. It is always important to try to start by defining the criteria by which the verdict in an essay is going to be judged and this candidate does this briefly and very effectively (the number of reforms, the size of the problems solved and the future effects of Gladstone's legislation). I find very little to disagree with in the comments on the separate reforms but feel that they could have been grouped together more logically and that the views on the more important matters could have been developed more fully. The essay tends to slip at times into wondering whether it really was a great ministry and this is a legitimate question but not quite the one set here. This piece would probably initially be seen as an A grade approach but lacking the factual substance and the development of separate points to sustain that mark. A sound B grade perhaps?

Additional note: it would now be worth revising

▶ the links between the reforms and the motives that gave rise to them
▶ the limitations of the reforms.

This would ensure coverage of several different types of questions based on the same political material.

Question 2 – outline answer
How do you explain the scale of the Liberal victory in the 1906 election?

Introduction: give brief indication of the scale, make point it came after a long period of Conservative domination in which the Liberals had many problems.

Argue that the main reason for the scale of the victory arose from the weaknesses and the mistakes of the Conservatives, give examples, events in South Africa after Boer War and 'Chinese Slavery' gave Conservative imperialism a bad name, Nonconformist anger at 1902 Education Act brought them back to the Liberals, Irish Home Rule issue had gone off the boil. Above all Conservative split over tariff reform and Liberal skilful exploitation of it in the election campaign (give examples).

Suggest that the Liberals offered few positive reform proposals: some promises to reverse recent anti-trade union court decisions were the most important. Their future pension and insurance reforms played no part in the election.

Conclusion: this was not one of the century's great 'swings to the left' and an agenda for radical reforms. Largely a negative victory, a reaction against long years of Conservative rule.

Solutions
British domestic history 1914–51

SOLUTIONS TO REVISION ACTIVITY

Politics between the wars

(a) The dates of elections are given in the Useful Information section of the Topic Outline but it is important that you are able to comment on the figures and apply them to essay questions. Use your textbooks to find out examples of the number of seats (and/or votes) gained by each party and think how to relate this information to such issues as Liberal decline, Conservative dominance and the rise of Labour.

(b) You will need to include why Lloyd George ceased to be trusted by the Conservatives (Chanak, deals with the Irish nationalists, the sale of honours, his earlier destructive effect on the Liberal Party) and the fears of many of their back-benchers that he would destroy the party system.

(c) Consider this as an answer: 'The formation of the National Government in 1931 had its origins in the financial collapse beginning with the Wall Street Crash of 1929. The financial strains imposed on the minority Labour Government by increased unemployment payments and declining economic activity caused great concern to financiers and speculators who began to threaten the stability of British currency. Unless confidence was restored it seemed likely that foreign speculators would start to transfer their sterling into gold and run down the country's gold reserves. This was talked up into a major crisis in which the government was given few options except reducing its debts in order to restore financial confidence quickly. It was the failure of the Labour cabinet to agree on suitable economies that first drove the Prime Minister, MacDonald, to resign and turned the financial crisis into a political crisis which was only resolved by creating a coalition government with the Conservatives and the Liberals.'

(d) How would you extend and improve this attempt? 'In the end Conservative domination of political life owed most to Baldwin's skill in defusing crises and reassuring the British people that all was well, as he did in 1926, 1931 and 1936. With him in control extremists on either flank were outmanoeuvred and the Labour Party was kept in its minority place. Over a succession of issues he convinced the British electorate that in a dangerous world their own and the country's safety was best ensured by voting Conservative.'

ANSWERS TO PRACTICE QUESTIONS

Essay Questions

Question 1 – student answer
Examine the view that fighting the First World War, rather than events after the war, brought about the end of the British Liberal Party.

(Warning note: this is presented as an example of a poorly organized essay)

Many historians believe that the First World War accelerated the decline of the Liberal Party because of the splits that took place. However up until 1929 the liberals still had a great chance of winning an election. It could therefore be argued that the

World War knocked the liberals down to such an extent that they could never recover as the party in office.

It can be argued that the Liberals didn't have a chance of winning an election after 1918. Firstly this is because of the World War. Many historians feel that the war was the time when the Liberal Party was forced into decline. This is because the strands of liberalism had virtually been broken. The liberal ideas of free trade, pacifism, non-intervention had to be dropped because of the war. Possibly the item that split the liberals the most was conscription. Liberalism entails freedom of the individual but they still forced men between the ages of 18 and 41 to enter the army.

The World War also caused a rift among the two leading politicians in the Liberal Party, Lloyd George and Asquith. This rift which carried on until 1924 left the Liberals divided into two sections. It could be argued that this is really what broke the Liberal Party. Other legislation and activities such as the defence of the Realm Act, the treasury agreement, the heavy handed budgets of 1914 and 1915 in which Lloyd George raised income tax to allow for expenditure during the war all helped to accelerate Liberal decline.

However it could be argued that the decline occurred after 1918 even more. This is because wealthy businessmen moved their funds from the liberals to the Conservatives. They had lost their faith in the Liberals to win an election and therefore pulled out their funds. This meant that the Liberal Party couldn't put up as many seats as they would have liked and therefore had to suffer a loss in seats.

It can also be argued that Lloyd George also accelerated the decline of the liberal party. It can also be argued that the Liberals may have had a better chance of winning the 1929 election if they hadn't had Lloyd George as their leader. This is because Lloyd George had become a very untrustworthy politician because he didn't fulfil his promises of 1918. For instance he promised 'a land fit for heroes' yet the economy declined and there was massive unemployment (it reached two million in July 1921). People had also lost trust in him because of the honours scandal when it was reported that Lloyd George was selling knighthoods and peerages in order to raise money for his own political fund. These meant that Lloyd George as leader in 1929 was an electoral liability. The Liberal decline after 1918 wasn't helped by the rise in the amount of women voters. The Representation of the People Act 1918 had given the vote to women over the age of 31. But a lot voted Conservative and many working-class people turned to Labour.

I agree with the view that it was the First World War rather than events after 1918 that destroyed the Liberal Party but it should also be taken into account that the liberals still had a possible election victory in them. For instance there was a revival in support at the 1929 election and therefore it could be argued that the World War simply made it more difficult for the liberals to recover because of the deep rooted splits that had erupted during the First World War.

Examiner's comments Phew! The opening is one of the most confused I have ever seen and, throughout, the candidate cannot arrive at a conclusion without immediately adding the other side of the arguments. You may not learn a lot on how to answer this particular question from reading this attempt but a close study of it could show you all sorts of pitfalls to avoid in the pressure of the examination. Think about the following organizational points:

▶ The candidate might have done much better if he had come down on one side or the other about the view in the essay title.

▶ If he agreed with the title he should then have taken first the war period and indicated its effects (he has some good ideas on this even if they are never really driven home) and explained why the party was fatally wounded in 1918.

▶ He seems however (despite twice stating the opposite!) to see events after the war as important. Then he should have started by arguing that the party still had a chance in 1918 (explain why) and take the period after the war and show what went wrong.

If this topic interests you as an examination choice you should start from scratch and work out your own, much clearer, plan of how to answer the question but it would still pay you to look again through this essay and ask yourself what you would do to improve the writer's answer. This is quite typical of too many student answers. The essay may need more substance (e.g. why voters started to switch to the Conservatives and to Labour in the 1920s is worth a paragraph and the fact that the Labour Party was strong enough to form a government in 1924 surely suggests how serious the plight of the Liberals was by then) but more crucially it cries out for better direction of the ideas and facts that it contains in order to answer the question. This student failed to use what he knew to any real effect. Would it surprise or encourage you to know that the examiner who marked it thought it had enough relevant points to place it in A-level grade D?

Question 2 – essay plan
How successful was the Labour government from 1945 to 1951 in solving the economic problems it encountered?

▶ First list the problems encountered: exhausted post-war economy, need for capital investment, how to pay for food imports, abrupt end of Lease Lend, loss of overseas investments, depleted shipping fleet, an overvalued pound.

▶ Argue that despite the winter of 1947 and the devaluation of the pound these problems were easing by 1949. Develop theme that nationalization was beginning to deliver capital investment and rationing and planning procedures were allocating resources to export industries and export trade. Later criticism that too much was spent on welfare measures at expense of economic investment was not true. It was Cold War rearming and particularly the Korean War that produced a new crisis of resources which wrecked the economic recovery.

Document question

Question 3 – the 1926 General Strike

(a) Sympathy strike of TUC to support miners interpreted by Conservative government as a constitutional threat, lasted ten days in May 1926.

(b) (i) Purpose was to rally support for the government by appealing to patriotic sentiment and by putting the strikers in the wrong in contrast to the reasonable and lawful approach of himself.

(ii) The means employed centre on his warlike vocabulary to evoke a crisis, e.g. 'government fighting', 'force Parliament', 'bend to its will', all of which emphasize the extremism of his opponents which he then contrasts with his own moderation, 'man of peace' and yet a man whom people can rely on vigorously to protect national interests; 'I will not surrender the safety and security of the British Constitution' is a direct appeal to patriotic sentiment.

(c) The central issue is whether the strike is purely an economic matter (extract II) or an attack on the constitution (extract I). They do differ as widely as seems possible but note the significant concession in extract II where the speaker concedes that some strike supporters would welcome it taking a revolutionary turn. It may well be worth commenting that perhaps both speeches, and certainly extract I, are propaganda statements where, for the sake of effect, extreme interpretations were adopted.

(d) This should, with 10 marks at stake, be a mini-essay at least one page long. Divide your answer into two equal parts to meet both parts of the question.

4 Solutions
British foreign policy 1815–1914

★ SOLUTIONS TO REVISION ACTIVITY

Castlereagh and Canning

(a) **Time-chart**
- ▶ 1815   Congress and Treaty of Vienna (see also pp. 41–3) Quadruple Alliance and Holy Alliance
- ▶ 1818   Congress of Aix-La-Chapelle
- ▶ 1820   Castlereagh's State Paper in which he resisted the idea of great states interfering as of right in the affairs of others, showing that he was closer to Canning's later policies than has been imagined
- ▶ 1820   Congress of Troppau: Castlereagh withdrew British delegates
- ▶ 1822   death of Castlereagh: Canning Foreign Secretary
- ▶ 1822   Congress of Verona to deal with events in Greece and Spain: collapse of the Congress system
- ▶ 1821–30   Greek independence
- ▶ 1823   recognition of independence of the Spanish South American colonies
- ▶ 1827   death of Canning

(b) **Essay plan**
- ▶ *Introduction*: agree that there was much continuity.
- ▶ Explain that Castlereagh had been responsible during the war period and was influenced by the turmoil of the French Revolution. He was prepared to work with continental powers to maintain peace but there were limits to this.
- ▶ Argue Castlereagh not all that much a reactionary, use refusal to join Holy Alliance, State Paper and Troppau withdrawal to illustrate this (some detail needed on this), as war receded he moved away from close cooperation with the continental countries.
- ▶ Then look at Canning. There was a difference of emphasis: in Spain, Spanish colonies and Greece he more vigorously pursued British interests.
- ▶ *Conclusion*: Castlereagh had already begun to change the emphasis of foreign policy.

(c) The continuity of principles in foreign policy between Castlereagh and Canning is indeed quite striking. Both sought British interests as their first priority. Castlereagh worked under the shadow of a disruptive revolution and a generation of war. He therefore saw British best interest as securing peace by trying to cooperate with the great continental powers whom British public opinion increasingly saw as reactionary despotisms. Canning, after 1822, worked in a more stable Europe and so could afford to risk quarrels with the other powers in order to assert specific British interests in Spain, Greece and South America. Some of Castlereagh's last policy moves suggest however that he was already moving in this way.

(d) Events to refer to include Castlereagh and Congress of Vienna, Holy Alliance, State Paper, Troppau withdrawal, Canning and Spain, Spanish colonies and Greece. Most of the factual detail will come from Castlereagh to support the idea that his ideas were changing towards those later followed by Canning.

ANSWERS TO PRACTICE QUESTIONS

Essay questions

Question 1 – student answer

Explain why Britain entered into so many foreign policy obligations to other countries in the period 1902 to 1914. How far do you agree that these commitments made its entry into the First World War inevitable?

The extent to which Britain in the late nineteenth century isolated itself from continental Europe can easily be exaggerated but it is true that, throughout the century, it avoided firm commitments which would automatically have brought it to the aid of other countries. Britain felt that its own interests, including its empire, were protected by the strength of its navy.

This situation changed very rapidly right at the end of the century though the origin of the change went back to the unification of Germany into one state in 1870. British policy towards Europe had always been based on the principle that no one power should become so powerful that it could dominate the continent. German union and the rapid industrialization that followed threatened to upset that balance. It was when Britain became increasingly aware of that danger that it became interested in alliances with other nations to protect its interests against the new danger. Several things around 1900 alerted Britain to the possible threat from Germany.

From 1898 Germany through a number of Navy Laws started to build an ocean-going navy of heavy battleships and in 1906 started to deepen the Kiel Canal so that they would have a totally safe anchorage in the event of war. This development caused great alarm in Britain and led popular newspapers to demand expansion of the British navy. From 1900 Germany was seen as the national enemy, replacing both France and Russia as the great continental threat. Germany had a large conscript army, now it had a navy. It was already a great industrial nation which was a trade rival to British industry in many fields. German political actions made the threat more real. At the time of the Boer War, 1899–1902, the German Kaiser was openly sympathetic to the Boers and as the war dragged on this irritated the British more and more. Later German attempts to bully France about North Africa backfired because they drove the British government to support the French and so encouraged closer ties between those two countries. These crises provoked a lot of anti-German feeling and tension.

The search for allies came because Britain began to feel insecure as Germany became more powerful. The insecurity was highlighted by the difficulties of the Boer War when it took three years and an army of a quarter of a million men to defeat two tiny Boer Republics. During the war Britain had no friends: European countries all sympathized with the Boer farmers fighting gallantly against British bullying though none moved to help them. This isolation made the British government realize that it would have great difficulty in defending its empire if it ever became involved in a European war. The war also worried Britain because so many of the men who volunteered to fight in Africa were too unfit to be taken into the army. Britain seemed unable to defend its possessions. From then on there was a lot of talk about the need to build up the army and navy and generally to make the country stronger so that it could stand up to other nations. The ideas of Social Darwinism were common at the time and they suggested that nations were rivals and only the strong would survive.

So from 1900 Britain began to look for allies. First it was the Japanese alliance of 1902 which was intended to provide Japanese defence of the empire in Asia if Britain got involved in a war in Europe. This alliance was as much against any Russian threat as a German one but it showed that the British had learned the lesson of the Boer

War that the world-wide empire needed allies if it was to be defended when Britain was involved in any European war. The entente of 1904 with France was much more in answer to the German threat to both nations and led the two countries to end their colonial rivalry in Africa. The way was now open for them to move closer together and soon their military leaders were involved in joint discussions on how to deal with any threat. It was the French who then encouraged the British to overcome their outdated suspicions of Russia and, again influenced by the obviously growing power of Germany, to come to an 'understanding' with its old enemy in 1907.

So, in answer to the first part of this question, Britain entered into alliances after 1900 because its security and its complacency about the navy protecting its interests were undermined by the growing threat it saw coming from Germany.

The second half of this question is more difficult to answer. Britain could in August 1914 have avoided entry into the First World War by ignoring its understanding with France. The Liberal Cabinet hesitated and it was the German invasion of Belgium, for whose neutrality Britain had been a guarantor since 1839, which enabled the war party in the Cabinet to push their colleagues into a declaration of war on Germany. To this extent there was nothing inevitable about it and Italy indeed ignored far more binding alliance ties to Germany and remained neutral until in 1915 it joined the war, not on the German but the Allied side. In the days before Britain came into the war the French government and the French ambassador in London were terrified that Britain indeed intended to remain neutral and used all the diplomatic pressure they could to prevent this.

In the end Britain probably had very little choice but to go to war sooner or later. The evidence of the 1870 war suggested that Germany was capable of winning an outright victory over France and then Britain would have faced a Europe dominated by the power it had come to distrust. Britain would then have had no allies available and the most important principle of its foreign policy would have been destroyed. It was not the understandings that made war inevitable but the fact that if Britain betrayed those understandings it would face an ever more powerful Germany on its own. In the end this would have forced it to war to protect France from total defeat.

> **Examiner's comments** This is a well-argued effective essay. Both parts of the very large question are answered though not at equal length. It is likely that the examiner will have some discretion to move marks from one part of the question to the other. Probably to the extent of marking one part out of 15 and the other part out of 10. It is essential that an answer is offered to both parts of double-barrelled questions like this. The candidate has offered opinions backed by reasons and is likely to be rewarded by an A grade for this answer.

Question 2 – essay plan
'Throughout the century from 1815 to 1914 it was relatively easy for Britain to secure its foreign policy objectives in Europe.' Discuss.
The most easily sustained argument is to claim that this is a greatly exaggerated claim.

▶ Agree that it was easier in the first half of the period, quoting Belgian independence, Greek independence and the Don Pacifico affair as examples of relatively easy victories. But even in this period Britain had to negotiate and compromise, e.g. allowing Austrian intervention in Italy and French in Spain in the Congress period. Crimean War was essentially futile and showed limits of Britain's ability to check Russia; similarly in 1878 Russia was checked by Disraeli only because Prussia and Austria wanted it so.

▶ Argue that after 1870 Britain had less influence in Europe (mention that even Palmerston in 1860s could not help the Danes against Prussia or the Poles against Russia). The Prussian defeat of France and German unification in 1870 changed the political balance in Europe and by 1900 put Britain on the defensive for the rest of the period to 1914, searching for allies and rearming in the face of the growing power of Germany.

Document question

Question 3 – Palmerston's foreign policy

(a) The claim of the British citizen, though he had few connections with Britain, against the Greek government for damages to his business caused by Greek rioters in Athens. There were serious doubts about how genuine the claim was.

(b) Extract I shows Palmerston's assertiveness and willingness to use force and should be quoted. The extract II critical reference to his bullying should also be referred to and his own strongly patriotic tone in extract III needs to be commented on. Note that this question clearly asks for information in the extracts so this is not the place to go on to use own knowledge from outside the extracts.

(c) Again it is evidence in the extracts that is wanted. Extracts II and IV provide the answer. Briefly quote both to show his general popularity. Then point out that many people close to politics appear to be less enthusiastic, mention the tone of extract II and the idea expressed there that 'Palmerston . . . will as usual escape unscathed' which implies contempt for him. Then note the considerable list of important opponents of Palmerston in extract IV, though its sweeping nature perhaps suggests that the writer may be exaggerating in order to emphasize her own disapproval of Palmerston.

(d) A historian would want to know how well informed the writers were likely to be on the events about which they write (were they there at the time and close to the events?) and whether they could be relied on in terms of their own political prejudices. With memoirs (extract II) it is useful to have some idea when they were written; with diaries the issue of later publication or alteration needs to be considered.

(e) For 10 marks this needs to be a mini-essay which must use both the extracts and own knowledge. When using the extracts quote from them, or summarize the point they make, but also explain in your own words what the point is that you think they establish. Indeed it is probably better to make your own point: 'Britain's role in Europe relied heavily on the supremacy of its navy. In extract I for example we see that the navy is in force in the Eastern Mediterranean, apparently visiting the very important strait between the Mediterranean and the Black Sea. Britain did not hesitate to use this power to enforce its interests even on minor nations like Greece and the order in extract I to take reprisals and blockade ports shows how ruthless Britain could be. There is no reference to any danger of opposition to the fleet so Britain can act as it wishes.' The other point that must be made is that some people in Britain were prepared to challenge these assumptions, then quote the extracts to illustrate this. Note that here you must bring in your own knowledge of the Don Pacifico affair as well. A strong answer will try to integrate own knowledge and extracts.

5 Solutions
British foreign policy 1914–70s

Britain's international position after the Second World War

(a) Consequences of the war included
  ▶ National Debt up from £8,000 million to £25,000 million, the loss of the bulk of overseas investments sold to pay for war supplies and a badly run-down industrial economy
  ▶ dependence on post-war US loans and then on Marshall Aid gave the USA the political initiative
  ▶ the election of a Labour government that was more inclined than the Conservatives under Churchill were to make concessions to those in India who wanted independence
  ▶ a devastated European continent half under the control of the Soviet Union again drove Britain to work to keep a US presence in Western Europe in order to check the further spread of communism
  ▶ a stimulus to national feelings for independence in Britain's Asian colonies in particular

After the war Britain's economy and military potential were dwarfed by the USA, its ability to act independently had been undermined. Attlee's Labour government accepted this and worked to support US resistance to the communist threat. Episodes worth following up are the decision to persuade the United States to take over Britain's work defending the Greek royalist government against communist rebels, to end the British mandate in Palestine, to grant India independence, to join the Korean War.

(b) **Time-chart**
  ▶ 1945   end of the Second World War
  ▶ 1946
  ▶ 1947   British India granted independence as India, Pakistan and Sri Lanka (Ceylon)
  ▶ 1948   Britain ended its mandate over Palestine
  ▶ 1949
  ▶ 1950   start of Korean War, heavy military expenditure
  ▶ 1951
  ▶ 1952
  ▶ 1953   Federation of Rhodesia and Nyasaland set up (dissolved 1963)
  ▶ 1954
  ▶ 1955
  ▶ 1956   Suez adventure ended in humiliation for Britain and France
  ▶ 1957   Ghana (Gold Coast) became independent. Malaya granted independence after successful war against communist forces
  ▶ 1958   West Indies Federation set up (dissolved 1962)
  ▶ 1959
  ▶ 1960   Cyprus and Nigeria both became independent
  ▶ 1961   Sierra Leone and Tanzania (Tanganyika) became independent
  ▶ 1962   (to 1966) independence of the separate West Indian islands recognized
  ▶ 1963   Kenya independent after long struggle against the Mau Mau
  ▶ 1964   Northern Rhodesia (Zambia) and Nyasaland (Malawi) became separate independent nations

- ► 1965 The Gambia became independent
- ► 1966 Guyana (British Guiana) became independent
- ► 1967
- ► 1968 Swaziland became independent
- ► 1969
- ► 1970 Fiji and Tonga became independent

(c) **Essay plan**

- ► *Introduction*: abandonment of empire was partly because of growing pressure in the colonies for independence and partly owing to changing circumstances in Britain and in Britain's role in the world. Once the abandonment started it built up its own momentum.
- ► Paragraph giving examples of national feeling in colonies causing increased problems of control for Britain – Indian nationalism, Palestine, Cyprus, Mau Mau in Kenya to be cited as examples.
- ► Britain after 1945 – to show why the empire became a burden better discarded: imperial defence already a problem in 1930s, unable to defend in war against Japanese, economy and finances crippled in the war, unable to maintain a world role.
- ► New age of the superpowers, US intolerance of Britain's imperial role, international weakness and dependence on USA clearly shown in 1956 Suez campaign, defeat here stimulated nationalist demands.
- ► There was a loss of will at home as shown by Labour's haste in India and Palestine and the Conservative rapid concessions in Africa and the West Indies in the 1960s. Britain preoccupied with social policies and difficult economic problems at home.
- ► The intellectual conviction that Britons had a right to rule much of the world had been lost: the end of empire was part of a wider process of European decolonization reflecting Europe's reduced status after the war and in an age of superpowers.

(d) The list of reasons is easy but it is their order of importance and the ability to comment on and illustrate them that will be more important in an examination.

- ► Britain had been fortunate not to be conquered in the Second World War and for this reason did not feel the same pressing need to be part of a European framework as did continental countries.
- ► Britons, even members of Attlee's Labour government, still saw themselves as a world imperial power; even Bevin the Foreign Secretary preferred cultivating the Commonwealth and the friendship of the United States to linking Britain to the devastated continental states.
- ► An island nation easily found an instinctive contempt for foreigners; this was a form of historical jingoism often found in the right-wing press based on an assumption of British superiority.
- ► Once joining Europe became a real possibility on economic grounds, then many felt threatened that aspects of national life which they valued would be swamped in a European super-state.

ANSWERS TO PRACTICE QUESTIONS

Question 1 – student answer
Examine the view that, from 1937 to 1939, appeasement of Hitler was a perfectly reasonable foreign policy for Chamberlain's government to pursue.

By 1937, if one believed Winston Churchill, the British government should have been able to see what Hitler was up to – domination of Europe by force. Germany was busily rearming and the Rhineland had, without opposition from France or Britain, been remilitarized, the payment of reparations had been denounced, all contrary to the terms of the Versailles Peace Settlement. This onward march of German power continued in 1938 with the Anschluss with Austria, also against Versailles, and the pressure on Czechoslovakia to hand over the Sudetenland. Chamberlain's government completely failed to stand up against these further acts of aggression but in cowardly fashion at Munich betrayed Czechoslovakia into German hands. Only in March 1939 did Chamberlain begin to change his tone, after Hitler had seized the rest of Czechoslovakia, with the introduction of conscription and guarantees to Poland. Churchill argued that Hitler had grown greedier with every failure to stand up to him and that the weakness of Britain and France had by 1939 made another European war to check Germany inevitable.

In this essay I will argue the contrary view and claim that Chamberlain's policy of appeasement, which ended in disaster, had still at the time much to be said in its favour. Churchill had at least opposed it at the time but most of those who later tore into Chamberlain only did so from hindsight and had been happy to support the government at the time.

Chamberlain believed that Hitler could be persuaded to act reasonably. He saw that Germany had legitimate grievances after the Versailles peace treaty and, along with many other English thought it unreasonable to expect a great power to accept such humiliations as reparations and the military bans. Even democratic German politicians like Stresemann had refused to accept the loss of lands in the east. Germany had reasonable claims to make and it was reasonable to assume that if these were met through diplomacy then the horrors of another war would go away. Many English people believed this so that, when the Rhineland was remilitarized by the Nazis, it was seen as the Germans just moving back into their own backyard and when in 1938 the Anschluss happened it was argued that they were all Germans anyway and that the people of Austria had clearly wanted union with Germany. With many people in Britain believing all this, especially right-wing supporters of Chamberlain's government, it would have been very difficult for him to 'stand up to Hitler' on these issues.

The opinions of the British people limited what Chamberlain could do, even if he had believed it right, in other ways. Following the First World War there was a strong pacifist feeling in the country with the Oxford debate on not fighting for your country and pacifist by-election strength being much quoted. People were afraid of the consequences of war when 'the bomber will always get through'. They had seen what happened to the cities of Spain and thought in terms of hundreds of thousands of civilians dead within the first few days of any war. It would have been impossible for any government to have led the country into war as the national terror and then the passionate relief at the time of Munich showed.

There were many other practical reasons which made a strong policy impossible and which suggested that concessions avoiding war were the best way forward. First the state of British defences which had been neglected in the 1920s, when Churchill had been Chancellor of the Exchequer, and early 1930s, were not ready for a war. Rearmament had started and key plans, like radar and fighter planes, had been laid but even in 1938 the plans were only beginning to be made reality, for example the radar network scarcely covered any of even the south-east coastline. Churchill's exaggeration of the scale of German rearming actually made the military gap between Britain and Germany seem worse than it was and made strong action seem even more impossible. It has been argued by some supporters of Chamberlain that the state of the defences in 1938 alone justified what was done at Munich. It bought time for the defence plans to become reality. It does however seem unlikely that Chamberlain was thinking in this way, he really wanted a permanent peace and believed he could get it. Nor does the catastrophe of 1940 suggest that the year's delay in the arrival of war was all that useful.

There were however many other good reasons behind what Chamberlain was doing. In view of the state of Britain's defences with any prospect of war we would have had to rely on allies being available to provide or support the resolute action which

Churchill wanted. In practice France, the obvious ally, was even weaker and more reluctant to take action than was Britain. Since the early 1930s it had hidden behind its new Maginot Line and had ignored its promises to the smaller countries of Eastern Europe. It did not have the will or the ability to launch an attack on Nazi Germany and nothing less would have deterred Hitler after the Rhineland had been reoccupied in 1936. The French could have prevented that but this can hardly be blamed on Chamberlain. The Dominions of the British Empire were equally lukewarm at the prospect of fighting another war in Europe when their own safety might be at risk if the Royal Navy was totally committed to the defence of Britain. The need to defend the empire during a European war was a massive problem for Chamberlain's government and made the avoidance of war, by appeasement, an attractive proposal.

A major disappointment for the British government was its failure to interest the USA and its president, Roosevelt, in the growing fascist menace in Europe. Roosevelt was an admirer of Europe but his domestic economic problems, the isolationist views of many Americans and his New Deal made him very reluctant to make any commitments and this did not change until war came. US isolationism left Britain alone to face the Nazis. The idea proposed later, that vigorous steps should have been taken to form an alliance with the Soviet Union, ignores the great distrust between the two countries and also that, after the Soviet purges, the military worth of a Soviet alliance was rejected by top British generals.

Chamberlain was a decent man and a much more active Prime Minister than has generally been appreciated. He sought peace because the country and the people were so unready for war. Any 'standing up' to Hitler was impossible without great military expenditure and without allies to stand with him. He was not a fool and early in 1939 he saw that his efforts were likely to fail and he was then prepared to take steps that had earlier been avoided. It was these steps, especially the guarantees to Poland, that marked the end of appeasement and which led both the Poles and Hitler to miscalculations that led to the outbreak of war. When war came it was at least a united country that went into it. This would not have been so in 1938. Only one part of Chamberlain's foreign policy was seriously mistaken and this was not the attempted appeasement of Hitler. He should have pursued a military deal with the Soviet Union much more vigorously though even here it is a fair question to wonder how far Stalin could have been trusted to honour any pact.

Examiner's comments This is a well-argued essay and one packed with relevant ideas. The charge against Chamberlain was skilfully set up and at reasonable length. Some students spend so long recounting the argument they propose to challenge that this begins to take over the essay. The directness of the attack on the question and the range of perceptive comments suggest that this essay deserves an A grade. One or two points do however need to be introduced in the essay to make it a full account:

▶ Britain's economic problems and social policies following the Great Depression were also a reason for not getting involved in a dangerous foreign policy or heavy military expenditure.

▶ Churchill, almost Chamberlain's only front-line critic, had few supporters and a dubious personal political reputation as a warmonger who seriously exaggerated the scale of German rearmament.

▶ The opposition Labour Party were committed to peace and dealing with social problems as their first priority.

▶ More analysis of what happened at Munich and on the difficulties involved in giving aid to the Czechs. The lack of trust in the Soviet Union needs more but so does the willingness of other small countries to support Hitler's plundering of the Sudetenland, the role of the Poles did much to cause their own later problems.

▶ The weakness of the League of Nations needs a brief reference somewhere in the discussion of Chamberlain's lack of options.

Question 2 – essay plan

How far do you agree that, in the Cold War period from 1946 to 1950, the British Labour government had little choice but to back the policies of the United States?

▶ *Introduction*: Agree with the question entirely so far as the big issues of foreign policy were concerned. Britain was desperate that the Americans stayed in Europe and countered the threat that was seen to be coming from communism and Soviet imperialism. Britain, exhausted by war, could not do this alone.

▶ Take a series of instances where Britain followed the US lead in the Cold War – accepted Marshall Aid to rebuild its economy, took full part in the Berlin Airlift, helped form NATO, joined the Korean War.

▶ If interests appeared to differ, US pressure brought Britain in line – the outstanding example is probably the ending of Britain's Palestine mandate. This is not quite the full story for Britain at times was able to influence the US policies – cite the case of Greece which led directly on to the Truman Doctrine and where Britain had been involved against communist rebels until its resources were exhausted and it had to persuade the USA to take up the fight. Cite also the Churchill 'Iron Curtain' speech to show Britain arousing the USA to action. The Labour Foreign Secretary Bevin was the fiercest opponent of communism and the Soviets despite Labour's earlier belief that it could work with them.

▶ The fact is that two capitalist democratic states had many interests in common so it was only natural they worked together with the USA, as the more powerful, usually but not always, setting the pace.

6 Solutions
European history
1815–70

★ **SOLUTIONS TO REVISION ACTIVITY**

France 1815–70

(a) **Time-chart**
- ▶ 1815–30   Bourbon Restoration (Louis XVIII to 1824, Charles X 1824–30)
- ▶ 1830   Revolution overthrowing the Bourbons
- ▶ 1830–48   Reign of Louis-Philippe
- ▶ 1848   Revolution setting up the Second Republic, revolutions across Europe
- ▶ 1848–52   Second Republic and the rise of Louis Napoleon
- ▶ 1852–70   Second Empire (Napoleon III); the autocratic empire of the 1850s and liberalization in the 1860s, Napoleon's foreign policy.

Examination questions may appear on any of these topics. The best strategy is to revise all of them and remove the element of lottery on which question comes up. Much of your general knowledge of French history (for example on the radical tradition carried over from the first French Revolution and on the right-wing Bonapartist tradition carried on from Napoleon I) will be of use in answering questions from anywhere in the period so try to make maximum use of this material. There is perhaps least to say on the 1830 Revolution and you should revise it with the possibility in mind of a question linking 1830 with 1848. Napoleon III is the biggest single revision topic.

(b) This is a simple exercise to encourage use of your textbook to make a chronological list of key words that will summarize the content. You can then apply this to activities (c), (d) and (e).

(c) The causes of the 1830 revolution not only involve the increased unpopularity of Charles X's policies but also include some account of how the 1789–1815 period had created a revolutionary tradition in France which burst out again in 1830. What sort of people opposed the Bourbons, who were lukewarm? In the second part of the question, the obvious consequence was the overthrow of the Bourbons but, after moderate middle-class politicians seized the initiative, it was replaced by another monarchy that simply followed more moderate policies. The revolution became a compromise. It provided constitutional government and protection of middle-class interests but did not meet the aspirations of the growing working class of Paris. In this way it led on to the 1848 Revolution.

(d) The republic survived such a short time because the people of France, and especially Paris, were deeply divided as to what sort of a society they wanted to develop. Even as early as 1848 the working-class radicals were brutally suppressed by Cavaignac and this with the full support of the middle class. After that the ranks of those who had been happy to see the back of Louis-Philippe found it impossible to work together. Fearful of socialism the 'respectable' classes in French society moved swiftly to the right politically and this worked to the advantage of Louis Napoleon who, as heir to Napoleon I's tradition, was able to appeal to all those who wanted stability and to those who sought a return to glorious policies. The other parties of the right, the royalist parties, were as divided as those who favoured a republic and Louis Napoleon was able to gain power by popular consent by exploiting the French people's desire to avoid a drift into anarchy.

(e) **Essay plan**
  ▶ Define French national interests in nineteenth-century terms: security from foreign attack, a balance of power in Europe, develop a French empire, return to the days when French influence and power was important in European affairs. (This may look quite vague but it is better than ignoring the issue.)
  ▶ Argue that the early policies were in French interests – checking Russia in the Crimean War protected France as a Mediterranean power, both French Catholics and liberals approved, also useful alliance with Britain – the interest in Italy provided a possible new ally and checked the Austrians, also gained Nice and Savoy.

ANSWERS TO PRACTICE QUESTIONS

Question 1 – student answer
How far do you agree that foreigners were more important than Italians in bringing about the unification of Italy?

The short answer to this question is that the activities of some Italians and some foreigners were both important to gaining Italian unification. The ideas of Mazzini, the political skill of Cavour and the military daring of Garibaldi were all essential. So were the help of the French Emperor Napoleon III and to a lesser extent the activities of both Britain and Prussia. Even the eventual decisions of both the Austrians and of the Italian pope to accept the inevitable played their part.

It seems unlikely that without some movement for unification among Italians since the beginning of the century that union would have come. Here the nationalist ideas of Mazzini were important and he became the inspiration for later nationalist movements. The revolts of 1848 failed in practical terms but it convinced Italian nationalists that they had to look to the one constitutional Italian state Piedmont to lead the move to unity. The republican idealists had failed, the pope had turned his back on them. After 1848 the Italian state of Piedmont was central to unification and without Piedmont it is unlikely that foreigners would have intervened to help bring it about. The work in Piedmont of the king Victor Emmanuel and of the Prime Minister Cavour in modernizing the state, building up its economy, administration and army made it fit to lead a move towards unification. It became the state that all Italian nationalists looked to lead unification

It was Cavour too who at the Pact of Plombières made the crucial moves to involve the French in ridding Italy of the Austrians. In this way the basis of unification owed much to Italians. Cavour himself had more limited aims, chiefly the expansion of Piedmont's control in northern Italy, but whatever he intended his actions started off a bigger movement which ended with a united Italy.

It is true however that unification was, in important ways, greatly assisted by foreign intervention. Most important was the active help of Napoleon III of France which drove the Austrians out of Lombardy and so weakened their power to interfere everywhere else in Italy. The Austrians were bluffed into attacking Piedmont and this gave France the excuse to send troops into Italy where they won two costly battles at Magenta and Solferino after which the Austrians had to hand over Lombardy to Piedmont. Napoleon then helped to persuade the people of three other states, Tuscany, Parma and Modena, to hold plebiscites and vote to become part of Piedmont. These gains made Piedmont the most important Italian state and none of it could have been done without the work of the French army. Napoleon however failed to carry out all the Pact of Plombières and drive the Austrians out of Venetia. He also claimed his reward and Piedmont had to hand over Nice and Savoy to France.

Italian unification could have ended there but for the actions of Garibaldi, and Italian nationalists who led a revolutionary expedition to Sicily to help an uprising started there by Mazzini. This expedition got so much support that it captured the island and then invaded the mainland of southern Italy and overthrew the ruler of the kingdom of Naples. It was only after this that Cavour decided he had to take control of the situation or an independent state might be set up in southern Italy with the republicans Mazzini and Garibaldi in control. The Piedmont army took over the Papal States in central Italy and moved south to help Garibaldi finish off the king of Naples. Garibaldi accepted Victor Emmanuel as the king of Italy and all the lands he had conquered as well as the Papal States conquered by the Piedmont army were joined to Piedmont as parts of the new kingdom. All this was confirmed by plebiscites held in the new territories in which large majorities voted to join Italy.

All of this great increase in size changed the earlier expansion of Piedmont in northern Italy into a real Italian kingdom and it had all been done by Italians. The only foreign help had been from the British navy which had been in the area of the Sicily landings. It did not help Garibaldi directly but its being there discouraged the navy of the kingdom of Naples from attacking Garibaldi's ships. France remained neutral in all this and Austria no longer had the power to interfere and stop the overthrow of the kingdom of Naples.

The union of Italy was not quite complete at this time. The pope still controlled the city of Rome which was the obvious capital city for a united Italy and the Austrians still occupied Venetia. The new Italian army was badly organized and led and was unlikely to be able to defeat the Austrians on its own. It was a military pact with Prussia which gave the Italians control of Venetia. In 1866 Italy followed Prussia in declaring war on Austria and although the Italian army did very badly in the fighting the total victory of the Prussians gave them their agreed reward and Venetia became part of Italy.

The problem in Rome was that, since the defeat of the 1848 revolution there, the pope had been protected by a French garrison. Napoleon III relied on the support of Catholics in France and could not withdraw his troops. Italy could not risk a war with the power of France and so it was stalemate. Again it was Prussian victories which helped the Italians when in 1870 France was at war with Prussia and had to withdraw its Rome garrison. After France was totally defeated by the Prussians the Italian army occupied the city. So in both 1866 and 1870 it was the actions of a foreign power, Prussia, that allowed the unification of Italy to be completed.

In conclusion it can be argued that the essay title is misleading in part or at least exaggerated. Without the force of Italian nationalism created by Mazzini and used by Garibaldi there would have been no wish for a united Italy. Also without the ambition of Cavour and Victor Emmanuel, who were both Italians, foreigners like Napoleon would not have become involved. The conquest of Naples was entirely Italian. At important stages in the unification foreigners did help, especially Napoleon in removing the powerful opposition of Austria, and less directly Prussia over Venetia and Rome. So foreigners were important at times but Italians played a larger part than this essay title suggests.

> ***Examiner's comments*** This essay provides an excellent example of how to ensure that a chronological descriptive account can be transformed into a very effective answer simply by providing a great number of comments which relate directly to the terms of the question set. This directness, which is backed only by standard rather than extensive knowledge, makes this at least a B grade answer. One great merit of the answer is that due attention is given to both the Italian and to the foreign contributions to unification. The essay is well organized and has a clear, directly relevant conclusion. It is a pity that the candidate omitted any consideration of Cavour committing Piedmont to fight alongside Britain and France in the Crimean War in order to win their support for Piedmont's ambitions against Austria. This episode surely best represents how Italian initiative and foreign assistance came together in the moves which eventually led to Italian unification. The price Italians had to pay for foreign help also deserves recognition, with the surrender of Nice and Savoy to France a particularly bitter blow to Garibaldi.

Question 2 – outline answer

To what extent was the unification of Germany a result of planning and to what extent a matter of chance and opportunism?

▶ *Introduction*: make the point that this question hinges on what view is taken on the role of Bismarck. It was once fashionable to see German unification as resulting from his ruthless pursuit of a master-plan. Argue in the essay that this was not the case.

▶ Bismarck did have a determination to build up the Prussian state as a first step to replacing Austria by Prussia as the dominant German state. He pursued this systematically from 1862 to 1866; give examples of his actions which support this view – probably best done by explaining how he isolated Austria from possible allies, especially Napoleon III before the 1866 war. Creation of the North German Confederation which followed was however Prussian expansionism, not a deliberate move to unification, and in 1866 Bismarck had no clear plans for further action.

▶ The great problem after 1866 was relations with France. Here Bismarck was more an opportunist than a planner. He schemed to put a pro-German candidate on the Spanish throne but did not plan a war with France. It was French overreaction (explain) that gave Prussia the opportunity in 1870 to attack and defeat a potential enemy. Bismarck then took advantage of Prussia's victory to negotiate with the south German states to turn the wartime military alliance into a more permanent political arrangement and the German Empire was born.

(*Note*: this is a theme that can be argued and supported – in an examination your plan would not be written out in this form or at this length!)

7

Solutions
European history
1870–1914

★ SOLUTIONS TO REVISION ACTIVITY

The Eastern Question

(a) Your list on the Congress of Berlin should include:
- ▶ The origins of the 1877–78 crisis including the weakness of the Ottoman Empire, the ill-treatment of the Christian inhabitants which gave Russia a reason to intervene militarily and the scale of the Russian advance which alarmed Austria-Hungary (why?). Leading up to the Treaty of San Stefano.
- ▶ The role of Bismarck and why he had to become involved because of his two allies heading for conflict; also why Britain (Disraeli) felt that it had to be involved.
- ▶ The terms agreed at the Congress to check Russian expansionism and an assessment of how successful these were in checking Russia and in lessening the tension in the Balkans (the conclusion could well be 'not satisfactory in either respect' but you need to be able to elaborate).

(b) Simply look at the Topic Outline again and use a standard textbook to supplement the map. Unless you are confident about why the great powers continued to interfere in the Balkans (i.e. their national interests there) you will never understand the complex detail of the Eastern Question or the causes of the First World War.

(c) Obviously you need to know what happened in each instance but these crises will often be only a small fragment of a wide essay on the origins of the First World War so you must have available a brief explanation of their importance:
- ▶ *Bosnian Crisis 1908* The Austrians 'got away' with the annexation of Bosnia and the Russians had to back down in their support of Serbia thanks to Germany backing Austria. This made the Austrians more determined in 1914, and more confident of German backing once more, hence their unreasonable pressure on Serbia. Russia, humiliated in 1908, could not afford to back down again in 1914 and retain any credibility in the Balkans and especially with the fellow Slav state of Serbia. All this made great power involvement much more difficult to avoid in 1914.
- ▶ *Balkan Wars 1912–13* These were settled without great power military involvement which seemed a hopeful sign for the future but in practice was not. The wars led to the expansion of Serbia which alarmed Austria-Hungary with its large Slav population. Austria was unlikely to stand aside again and see further Serbian expansion. On the other hand, the diplomacy of the great powers had frustrated the Serbian dream of access to an Adriatic port. Serbian expansionist ambitions had been encouraged but far from satisfied. This, and Serbia's relationship with Russia, was the key ingredient in bringing about the 1914 conflict.

✎ ANSWERS TO PRACTICE QUESTIONS

Question 1 – student answer
How far do you agree that there is 'much to be said for the view that Germany brought about the First World War'?

This verdict over-simplifies the 1914 situation but is basically correct. Germany's unification in 1870 upset the European balance of power and, although for the next twenty years Bismarck worked to maintain peace in Europe, clumsy German diplomacy after 1890 encouraged the development of the two rival alliance systems. The immediate cause of the war, in the Balkans, was not directly a German concern but Germany can be blamed for expanding the Balkan crisis into first an east European war and was then totally responsible for its expansion into western Europe. If the view in the essay title is correct then this arises largely from Germany's strong 1914 support for Austria against Serbia and then from its ruthless implementation of the Schlieffen Plan against France. These actions turned a Balkan crisis into a general east European crisis involving Russia and then transformed this into a general European war.

Germany's power in central Europe was unavoidable after its unification and because of its rapid industrialization. The total defeat of France in 1870 left the French seeking revenge and Germany's close links with Austria were always likely in the end to antagonize Russia. This formed the basis of the future rival alliance systems. It is hard to blame Germany for this situation which its very creation had made all too likely. More blame was due to the clumsy actions of Kaiser William II and his ministers after the dismissal of Bismarck which drew Britain into the Franco-Russian alliance through such actions as sympathizing with the Boers in the Boer War and setting out to build up a navy of heavy warships able to challenge Britain. This expanded the arms race which greatly increased international tension. Other German action which annoyed Britain was less blameworthy, such as its search for colonies in Africa and the Pacific or its growing export of industrial goods into British markets. The Kaiser was however much more to blame with his interference over French influence in Morocco for the closer links developed, including in military matters, between France and Britain and for a general increase in international tension before 1914. In this view Germany was chiefly responsible for the division of Europe into two hostile, and increasingly heavily armed camps. On the other hand the Germans could argue that they were not solely responsible and point to the way in which their security was threatened by their encirclement by France and Russia which would force them to fight a war on two fronts.

The German historian, Fischer, sees German responsibility for the outbreak of the First World War as centring on the support it gave to the Austrians in their 'bullying' of Serbia. He has argued that the Kaiser and the Chancellor, Bethman Hollweg, were both prepared to consider a war, which in any case they thought would be local and short, in order to break Allied encirclement and to end the threat posed by the Franco-Russian alliance of 1893. In all this they were urged on by Germany's military leaders, Ludendorff of the army and Tirpitz, who had created the navy. According to Fischer these men came close to meeting the Versailles charge that they were 'guilty' of causing the war. Many historians would agree at least to the extent that in the jingoistic atmosphere that built up before 1914 these men were prepared to take risks and to argue that Germany had to support its only reliable ally Austria. They did not try to restrain the Austrian government in its pressure on Serbia. Of course you can argue that Austria at this stage was even more responsible for what happened and it was Austrian guns that fired the first shots of the war by bombarding Belgrade.

It was Germany's facing up to the threats on Austria by Russia which first expanded the area of conflict. Germany demanded that Russia stop its troop mobilization and when it did not do so it declared war on Russia. It has been argued that Russia was only trying to put pressure on Austria to ease up on Serbia. If this was so then Germany's action in declaring war can be seen as the crucial first step in causing a war involving the great powers. The next step it took was even more clear-cut.

German war strategy was based on the Schlieffen Plan which assumed any war would be fought on two fronts, east and west, and that the German aim must be to knock out France quickly before Russia could get fully into the war. Germany made outrageous demands on France, including the surrender of its main border fortresses and when these were refused it declared war on France. This extension of the war into western Europe was entirely brought about by Germany's bullying and on its own goes a long way to support the title of this essay. Their chosen route to defeat France, by an attack through Belgium, made sure that Britain would not remain neutral. Germany's late promises that Belgium independence would be restored after the war were not enough. Britain had treaty obligations to protect Belgium and in any case could not stand by while the German army swept across France. The idea of a German-dominated Europe could not be accepted by the British and by not seeing this Germany's ambitious military strategy widened still further the course of the war.

In conclusion there is much to be said in favour of the view that Germany brought about the war. This is not quite the same as arguing that Germany was guilty of starting the war. It could not help its size and its strength or the fact that other powers were so frightened of it that they formed a hostile alliance against it. It made mistakes when it rushed into war with Russia and miscalculated about how Britain would act. It came nearest to deliberately starting a war when it backed Austria against Serbia in so full a way and its Schlieffen Plan greatly expanded the war. These two matters alone are enough to justify the view given in the title of this essay.

> **Examiner's comments** This is one of those answers, and they come along more frequently than cynics imagine, which make examiners wonder whether, in examination conditions, they could have done as well as the candidate. Its two great merits are that
> - ► it persists in giving a direct answer to the question right through to the last sentence and has no unnecessary descriptive material
> - ► it is packed with relevant ideas.
>
> It could be longer and so allow for more supporting information, perhaps on the political situation within Germany in 1914 and on the build-up of popular war hysteria, in Germany and elsewhere, as a major cause of the war. It could usefully have developed the argument that other powers were also in part responsible including
> - ► a reference to Serb terrorism in creating the original spark of violence
> - ► a deeper analysis of the mistakes made by both Austria and Russia.
>
> But in its directness and the quality of its ideas this is an A grade answer.

Question 2 – essay plan
To what extent was the existence of the system of alliances responsible for the outbreak of a general European war in 1914?

- ► *Introduction*: argument will be that the alliance system was not responsible for the outbreak of war in 1914 but that it was responsible for turning what could have been just another Balkan crisis into a general European war.
- ► Outbreak of war: analyse long-lasting Austro-Serbian rivalry going back to the Eastern Question of the nineteenth century. In 1914 this led to the first fighting but was not a result of the alliance system. Even the Russian mobilization was a traditional response to Austria in the region.
- ► The first stage of the spread of the war however occurred very largely because of the alliance system; analyse the crucial episodes: German backing of Austria, declaring war on Russia and then attacking France (though this was as much a result of German military strategy as of the alliance system).
- ► Britain's involvement stemmed from the entente with France but it came in only after Belgium was attacked. Could have avoided entry but could not see a German-dominated Europe. Nothing automatic about entry because of alliance; remember Italy never honoured its alliance with Germany.
- ► *Conclusion*: alliance system spread war from the Balkans because of Germany. Franco-Russian alliance spread it into Western Europe. Its main effect was to make the war spread so quickly that there was no chance for any one to pull back.

8 Solutions
European history 1914–45

Soviet Union

(a) Your list should include at least the following:
- ► October Revolution 1917 and the roles of Lenin and Trotsky in bringing it about (it is worth going back to April 1917 to note how Lenin pressed the Bolsheviks to speed up the seizure of power)
- ► closure of the Constituent Assembly when the Bolsheviks were in a minority
- ► central role of the Communist Party in the state
- ► use of the Cheka to terrorize opponents
- ► War Communism
- ► victory in the Civil War (especially the role of Trotsky)
- ► Treaty of Brest-Litovsk bringing peace with Germany at a great price
- ► switch to the New Economic Policy and its effects
- ► Lenin's ill-health and his failure to make clear decisions about the future leadership.

Preparing an assessment of Lenin will provide a clear theme for revision of this crowded period.

(b) **Essay plan**
- ► *Introduction*: explain purges fall into two very different phases – persecution of the kulaks to 1934 and the purge of suspected political and other leaders from 1936.
- ► Establish what happened to the kulaks to agree: use of 'ruthless' is totally justified.
- ► Argue that, from Stalin's point of view his collectivisation of Soviet agriculture (explain this) the destruction of the kulaks (independent peasants) was necessary.
- ► Briefly explain the scale of the later purges, numbers involved and range, including the army and quite ordinary people, again to agree that it was certainly ruthless. Here challenge whether they *were* necessary and argue these purges were the result of Stalin's paranoia and were not needed for the safety of the state or for the great economic changes being pushed through.

(c) If the millions of kulaks driven from their land and the millions who died of starvation in the agrarian purges of the early 1930s are added to the three million executed and the three million who died in concentration camps during the Great Purge from 1936 to 1939 then the ruthlessness of what happened is clear. The early purges of kulaks may have had an economic purpose and certainly, at enormous cost in suffering, they were part of the process of transforming Soviet agriculture. The later purges had no such rational purpose and occurred solely at the whim of the Soviet dictator and then took on a momentum of their own. Far from being necessary they inflicted great harm on both the economy and the military power of the Soviet Union.

(It is now worth thinking about how you would answer a question asking how great was the harm done to the Soviet Union by the purges.)

(d) Issues could include
- ► collectivization of agriculture
- ► Five Year Plans for heavy industry and the power industry, including the opening up of new industrial areas

▶ imposition of a command economy organized around Five Year Plans
prepared by Gosplan and marking the end of free market economics.
You will need specific information, including a few statistics of industrial growth
and the Five Year Plans, to give substance to an essay, because knowledge often
seems quite thin on economic topics like this. Comment too on the limits of
economic development with little expansion of consumer goods production and
the return in the late 1930s to heavy investment in military defence.

ANSWERS TO PRACTICE QUESTIONS

Question 1 – student answer
**'By 1934 Hitler had established his total control of the German state
and had done this by totally legal means.' Discuss.**
(You are urged to think about how you would answer this question before reading
the interesting but flawed answer which follows. Please then read the examiner's
comments carefully.)

There is no doubt that by 1934 Hitler had established his total control over
Germany. The Enabling Law allowed him to rule without the Reichstag, other political
parties than the Nazis were made illegal and opponents were ruthlessly pursued. The
real question is whether all this had been done by totally legal means.

During the early 1920s Hitler had tried to come to power by illegal means, as
witnessed by the Beer Hall Putsch of 1923. For this he was imprisoned and decided
that legal methods would have to be adopted. In fact he said 'if outvoting them
means out-shooting them then the result will be the same'.

The NSDAP entered the Parliamentary system and during the next few years were
only able to maintain a small presence in Parliament as the prevailing 'Golden Years'
caused extremist support to decline. However the Wall Street Crash precipitated a
huge crisis in Germany. The Muller government fell apart over the issue of what to do
about the problems of unemployment and no more loans – the DVP wanted less public
expenditure and the Socialists wanted more spending to create jobs. The Muller
government was the last majority government and collapsed in 1930.

A series of short-lived minority governments followed which depended on the
President's power to pass emergency decrees to survive. All the while the Nazi votes
were slowly creeping up. In the elections they steadily gained more and more seats
and they confined themselves to Parliamentary activities. After Chancellor Bruning
failed President Hindenburg prevailed upon Von Papen but he also failed and Von
Schleicher was called on to become Chancellor. But after he failed too he and other
right-wing politicians persuaded Hindenburg to offer the post to Hitler from which he
had so far withheld himself, even though the last election had in fact left the NSDAP
with 196 seats compared to 230 before.

Waites argues as is apparent, that Hitler's accession to power on the 31st Jan.
1933 was strictly constitutional without any trace of illegal practices. However, once
he was in power things began to look different. Despite having only Goering and Frick
as NDSAP members in the cabinet, Goering was Prussian Minister of the interior and
thus had enormous police powers. The Nazis began to abuse their power and
specifically raid communist headquarters and attack communists.

In late February a fire broke out in the Reichstag and a communist, Van den Lubbe,
was accused of setting it. As a result Hitler was able to pass the Decree for the
protection of the People and the State. If the Nazis actually rigged the fire they were
definitely guilty of using illegal means to gain a law that gave them more wide-ranging
powers of arrest and detention.

On the 5th of March elections were held, and the Nazis were definitely guilty of
illegally employing terror, intimidation and violence to frighten people into voting for

them. Nevertheless they still only got a majority with the Nationalists' support. Hitler then wanted to pass the Enabling Act which gave the Nazis absolute power for 4 years. This involved a change in the constitution and would require a majority of two-thirds. This was achieved also by illegal means – violence and terror, and many communists who would have voted against it were arrested and taken away. The meting in the Kroll Opera House found the walls lined with SA and SS men and the law was passed.

It can be argued that once the Enabling Act was passed anything the Nazis did was legal as they had absolute power, but (a) the very passing of the law was illegal because of the manner in which it was passed, and (b) was it intended to allow them to murder loot and pillage? From the passing of the Act the Nazis were free to do as they pleased – the communists who hadn't yet escaped were murdered and the persecution of the Jews began. The Night of the Long Knives in 1934 – the murder of all possible opposition to Hitler including Ernst Rohm leader of the SA – was an act of brutality. Was this legal because of the Enabling Act? Or did the Enabling Act only enable them to do what they wanted insofar as it was legal? If so then even what they did after it was passed was illegal.

Thus one can conclude that from 1929 to 1933 when he came to power Hitler did in fact employ legal methods. But the consolidating of his power was different altogether. The means used to win the March elections and the Enabling Act was definitely illegal and it is possible to argue that it was still illegal after the Enabling Act was passed. Therefore it may be true that his rise to power in 1933 was entirely legal, what happened afterwards through 1933 and 34 was not, although some of it was still legal.

Examiner's comments The central argument is sound – legal to January 1933 but more questionable after that. The student clearly also has reasonable knowledge of the topic and employs a good vocabulary and uses paragraphs in developing the points made. All this certainly makes it a D or, more likely, a C grade essay.
It could do better than this but it is weak in that

▶ In the long paragraphs 2 and 3 it describes what other politicians did and fails to focus on Hitler and it is misleading in claiming the steady advance of the party in elections and eventually this is contradicted.

▶ A closer focus is needed on what Hitler did in elections, with some dates and figures. Nazi use of propaganda was legal but were the SA election battles in the streets legal?

▶ The explanation of how Hitler came to power because of the intrigues of other right-wing politicians is rather muddled but the real point that should be made more firmly is that Hindenburg's appointment of him as Chancellor was entirely within the constitution.

▶ The questioning of the Enabling Act is not at all clearly expressed but it was passed by a large majority with only the Socialists voting against. It was certainly passed in dubious circumstances, among which this student fails to point out that the communists had been banned from attending the Reichstag.

▶ If less time had been spent describing pre-1933 politics more could have been made of the election held after Hitler came to power, this was before the Enabling Act was passed but the Nazis used all their control of the state and great intimidation of voters. Here the question of its legality is crucial.

▶ The student is surely right to question the legality of the Night of the Long Knives even under the Enabling Act. On a factual point however it was the SA who were the victims and not as stated 'all possible opposition to Hitler'. At this point the student does not seem to be in control of his facts.

▶ The random introduction of a historian's name adds nothing to the essay.

▶ The concluding paragraph starts very effectively but peters out in the last sentence.

Question 2 – essay plan

How far do you agree that fascist rule in Italy had, by 1939, brought substantial benefits to the country?

▶ *Introduction*: there may have been some minor benefit but basically there are few grounds for agreeing with this claim. Mussolini was a master of propaganda and this usually covered a thin record of worthwhile achievements

▶ Paragraphs on the major areas of alleged achievement:

   ▶ The economy, some slight gains from battle for grain but other crops reduced and land ownership not reorganized. Pontine Marsh drainage probably the one real achievement of the fascist period and even this had to be retrieved after wartime neglect. Industry under corporate state bureaucratically controlled to protect inefficient large Italian firms, with some advance in car manufacture and power supply but it is a myth that Mussolini created an efficient railway system. Much political corruption hindered small enterprises.

   ▶ Society, battle for births was a failure, state provision for leisure was for a minority, education still inefficient, no independent trade unions, opponents persecuted, authoritarian regime stifled initiative in any of the arts. Catholic Church kept its privileged position. Main social gain was the clamp down on the Mafia.

   ▶ Empire in Ethiopia brought only propaganda benefits. Nor did fascists create an efficient military (Italy unfit to join war in 1939). Worse, Mussolini tied Italy to Hitler's warlike aims and this led to disaster after 1939.

   ▶ *Conclusion*: perhaps the main fascist achievement was to end the pre-1922 political instability but they never built much on this. Instead Italian life was stifled under an authoritarian regime which was driven to foreign policy adventures in order to distract from growing disillusionment at home.

Part IV

Timed practice paper with solutions

HISTORY PRACTICE EXAMINATION PAPERS

It is very difficult to provide a specimen history examination paper which will meet the majority of circumstances. This is not only because different examination boards have different papers but also because, even within the same board, there is usually a range of option and outline papers with different requirements and regulations. It is therefore very important that you are able to see recent previous copies of the specific papers you will be taking. If the paper is completely new then, almost certainly, the examination board will have issued a specimen paper to examination centres. You need at least to see that – and well before the examination.

Nearly all the examination boards have two types of papers:

▶ **Outline paper** often covering several centuries of which you will probably have studied only one. The paper could have up to 40 or more questions, almost certainly in chronological order and usually limited to either British or European history. The questions almost always require essay answers. Often they do not span across the century but are in-depth questions on specific topics within the century. In this sense, the term 'outline' is misleading.

▶ **Option paper** on a narrowly defined topic, for example 'The Nazi State from 1933 to 1945' or, less narrowly, 'Europe of the Dictators 1919–39'. These papers are usually entirely British or entirely non-British history. Candidates who take an outline British paper usually have to take an option paper in non-British history and vice versa. All the examination boards are required to have questions based on the use of documentary evidence and they usually choose to attach these questions to the in-depth option paper.

With all these complications in the way that history is examined, it is scarcely possible to provide a model paper that would not in some important ways be misleading to some candidates. The practice paper that follows is a combined paper which gives two typical document questions and twenty essay questions. These and the examiner's comments that are provided should give you good practice in handling actual questions which appear on the papers. It is however not possible to duplicate all the different examination instructions which candidates will face, though two examples are given below.

Examination instructions

A typical example for an option paper might well read:

TITLE (e.g. British politics 1832–68)
Time available 3 hours
All questions are marked out of 25
Answer **both** questions from Section A and **any two** questions from Section B

Section A (two document questions)
Section B (eight or ten essay questions)

A typical example of an outline paper could read:

TITLE (e.g. European history 1763–1945)
Time available 3 hours
All questions are marked out of 25
Answer **any four** questions

It is essential that, well before the examination date, you familiarize yourself with the instructions for the papers you are about to take and that you carry these out to the full. Failure to do so could well mean that some of your answers will be disregarded. The good thing is that the instructions are usually brief and simple to follow.

▶ Now look through the practice paper that follows but remember that each of the two papers you will take in the actual examination will differ from it in important respects.

▶ Select questions on topics which you hope might come up in your actual examination and work out your own solutions before turning to the answers proposed below.

Consider attempting to answer at least one question in full within the normal time limit of 45 minutes.

TIMED PRACTICE PAPER IN MODERN HISTORY

Time 3 hours
Answer **ONE** extract question from Section A and any **THREE** questions from Section B
All questions are marked out of 25

Section A

Extract question 1 – The passing of the 1832 Parliamentary Reform Act
Study the three extracts below and then answer the sub-questions which follow:

Extract I

March 7th, 1831 Nothing talked of or thought of or dreamt of but Reform. Every creature one meets asks, What is said now? How will it go? What is the last news? What do *you* think? and so it is from morning till night, in the streets, in the clubs, and in private houses. . . .

   March 11th, 1831 It is curious to see the change of opinion as to the passing of this Bill. The other day nobody would hear the possibility of it, now everyone is beginning to think it will be carried. *The tactics of the Opposition have been very bad*, for they ought to have come to a division immediately, when I think Government would have been beaten, but it was pretty certain that if they gave time to the country to declare itself the meetings and addresses would fix the wavering and decide the doubtful. There certainly never was anything like the unanimity which pervades the country on the subject, and though I do not think they will break out into rebellion if it is lost, it is impossible not to see that the feeling for it . . . must prevail.

(*Original Source*: Memoirs of Charles Greville
of the Reigns of George IV and William IV)

Extract II

The Government carried their second reading of the [Reform] Bill by 1 in the fullest House ever remembered. We had 301 and they had 302. . . . Our hope now is to throw it out in the Committee: but the misfortune is that the Ministers have made the most unsparing use of the King's name and, having obtained his sanction to the

Bill, it becomes next to impossible to oppose all reform, which, after all, is the only principle to go upon. . . . Our difficulties in opposing reform are, however, all aggravated by Peel's character. If the Conservative Party felt that they could rely on him, they would fight the battle; but they cannot. . . . On the Government side the party are united, zealous, active and using every means to carry this mischievous Bill.

> (*Original Source*: Memoirs of Mrs Arbuthnot for 29 March 1831)
> (*Reproduced in*: Smith, EA, *Reform or Revolution,*
> *A Diary of Reform in England 1830–1832*, Alan Sutton, 1992)

Extract III

I must assert that the speech of the learned gentleman had points of weakness which no imprudence ever surpassed. . . . He warns the *Peers of England* to beware of resisting the popular will, and he draws from the fate of the French nobility at the Revolution the example of the folly of a similar resistance. Good God! . . . where has the learned gentleman lived . . . when he attributes the downfall of the French nobility to an . . . obstinate resistance to popular opinion? The direct reverse is the notorious fact.

> (J W Croker addressing the House of Commons,
> 23 September 1831, and replying to a speech by T B Macaulay)

(a) In the context of these extracts identify:
   (i) 'the Opposition' (extract I)
   (ii) 'the Peers of England' (extract III)   *(2)*

(b) In the context of these extracts what do you understand by 'The tactics of the Opposition have been very bad' (extract I)?   *(3)*

(c) To what extent are extracts II and III agreed in their views of the desirability of reform?   *(4)*

(d) What is the purpose of the speaker in extract III and how effectively does the language and tone of his speech promote his purpose?   *(4)*

(e) Noting the origins of these three documents, how highly should a historian, studying how the Reform Act was passed, value their evidence?   *(5)*

(f) From your own knowledge of the passing of the 1832 Reform Act, how satisfactory an account of how it was passed can be constructed from the evidence of these extracts alone?   *(7)*

> *(Total marks 25)*

Extract question 2 – The rise of the Nazis to power

Study the three extracts below and then answer the sub-questions which follow.

Extract I

During Hitler's struggle for power a large percentage of his followers were young people. Many young Germans had been disappointed by the revolution of 1918 and the events that followed. They believed that a thorough change in economic conditions was necessary, but the German democracy . . . was essentially conservative. . . . Lower middle-class idealists who regarded Versailles as a national humiliation were prone to dream about a strong Reich . . . and Hitler seemed to offer this. . . . Another section of German youth followed Hitler because he promised a social revolution which would at the same time be national. . . . a German revolution, a German socialism. Hitler promised a future, jobs, recovery, a new national honour.

> (Extract from an article in *The Nation*, an American newspaper, June 1936)

Extract II

At that time [1931] the party leadership held completely contradictory and confused views on economic policy. The Führer personally stressed time and again during talks with me and industrial leaders to whom I had introduced him, that he was an enemy of state economy and of so-called 'planned economy' and that he considered free enterprise and competition as absolutely necessary in order to gain the highest possible production.

> (From the evidence of Walther Funk, a leading Nazi politician, to the post-war Nuremberg tribunal. *Reproduced in*: Shirer, William L, *The Rise and Fall of the Third Reich*, Secker and Warburg, 1960)

Extract III

As I walked through the Berlin streets, the Party flag was everywhere in evidence. Huge posters, pictorial homilies and Nazi slogans screamed from windows and kiosks, blazoning forth messages about honour and duty, national solidarity and social justice, bread, liberty and the beauty of sacrifice – all proclaiming the consummate skill with which Hitler had been leavening the masses. Passers-by wore tiny lapel emblems; uniformed men elbowed their way through the crowd, the swastika circling their brawny arms.

I drove back to witness the great Grunewald Stadium rally which was to wind up the entire campaign. . . . By the time night began to steal over the field more than a hundred thousand people had paid to squeeze inside while another hundred thousand packed a nearby race-track where loudspeakers had been set up to carry Hitler's words. And at home millions were waiting at the radio, open to the Nazis for the first time in this campaign.

Inside the stadium the stage-setting was flawless. . . . a dramatic speaking stand . . . hung with giant swastikas. . . . Draperies likewise flaunting swastikas made a simple and thrilling background. Picked men from the Schutzstaffel were drawn up in close ranks below the stand. Twelve huge SA bands played military marches with beautiful precision and terrifying power.

> (Kurt Ludecke *I Knew Hitler*, published 1938, and describing the June 1932 Reichstag election campaign)
> (*Reproduced in*: Purnell, *History of the Twentieth Century*, **vol. 3**)

(a) In the context of these extracts what do you understand by
   (i) 'Versailles' (extract I)
   (ii) 'men from the Schutzstaffel' (extract III)?   *(2)*

(b) Why, according to extract I, did 'Many young Germans' prefer to support Hitler and the Nazis rather than the other political parties of the Weimar Republic?   *(4)*

(c) In what ways does the evidence in extracts I and II suggest that 'Hitler's promised social revolution' would not be easily realized?   *(5)*

(d) How effectively does the content, language and tone of extract III convey the nature of the popular appeal of the Nazi Party in the 1932 election campaign? *(4)*

(e) Noting the origin of each of these three extracts, suggest one reason in each case why a historian of the Nazi rise to power would wish to use their evidence with caution.   *(3)*

(f) From your own knowledge, how satisfactory an account of the Nazi rise to power can be constructed from the evidence of these extracts alone?   *(7)*

> *(Total marks 25)*

Section B

Answer any **three** questions from this section

British history

1 How effective a Prime Minister do you judge Lord Liverpool to have been from 1815 to 1827?

2 'First he created a new Conservative Party and then he destroyed it.' Discuss this verdict on Peel from 1832 to 1846.

3 How successful was Palmerston's conduct of foreign policy in advancing British national interests?

4 Examine the principles on which the work of Gladstone's ministry from 1868 to 1874 was based.

5 How far do you agree that Disraeli's achievements at home in his ministry from 1874 to 1880 were overshadowed by his work in foreign and imperial affairs?

6 Account for the emergence of the British Labour Party in the period to 1914.

7 Why did Britain go to war with Germany in 1914?

8 Why, in the period from 1914 to 1924, did the British Liberal Party collapse so totally?

9 How far do you agree that in the late 1930s a foreign policy based on appeasement of Hitler was a very sensible one for the British government to adopt?

10 'Britain has lost an empire but failed to find a role': discuss this comment on British foreign and imperial policy in the years from 1945 to the 1960s.

European history

11 'A settlement based on satisfying the interests of the Great Powers rather than on any political principles.' Discuss this view of the Vienna Peace Settlement of 1815.

12 To what extent can Charles X be held responsible for the downfall of the Bourbon monarchy in 1830?

13 Why was Europe so convulsed with revolutions in 1848 and why did so many of the revolts fail to achieve what those who revolted had intended?

14 How much did the successful unification of Italy, to 1870, owe to the Italians themselves?

15 To what extent can the unification of Germany be regarded as the work of Bismarck alone?

16 Why were international relations in the Balkans so tense in the 1870s and how successful was the Congress of Berlin in reducing those tensions?

17 Account for the division of Europe into armed camps in the period from 1890 to 1907.

18 Why, in the period 1922 to 1929, were the Italian fascists able to establish total control over the Italian state?

19 'The people gained great benefits but at the price of an almost total loss of individual freedom.' Discuss this verdict on Nazi Germany from 1933 to 1939.

20 'Without rational purpose and bringing great danger to the Soviet Union': how far do you agree with this verdict on Stalin's purges of the 1930s?

EXAMINER'S ANSWERS AND NOTES ON THE TIMED PRACTICE PAPER

Section A

Extract question 1 – The passing of the 1832 Parliamentary Reform Act

(a) (i) The Tories
    (ii) House of Lords

(b) The author of extract I thought that the Opposition should have acted immediately to block the Bill and forced a vote on it because he believed, though he does not give any evidence, that they would have won the vote. Because they did not do this the supporters of reform around the country had time to mount a great campaign, to persuade those who were uncertain, that they should support the Bill and also to give the impression that all the country wanted it. As a result it seemed to the author that the reform must be passed.

(c) Extracts II and III were largely agreed that reform was not desirable. Extract II writes of her 'hope' of throwing it out in committee and that it is a 'misfortune' that all reform cannot be opposed for it is a 'mischievous Bill'. Extract III is trying to urge the Lords to resist reform for it was the failure of the French nobility to resist that destroyed them. He describes the speech of a supporter of the Bill as being weak and very imprudent.

(d) The purpose of the speaker in extract III was first to undermine the previous speech of Macaulay in the Lords and by doing this to stiffen the resistance of the Commons, where he is speaking, to reform. He uses language to create a tone of amazement at Macaulay's naivety and lack of understanding of what really happened in the French Revolution and the lessons to be drawn from it. His claim that 'no imprudence ever surpassed' Macaulay's and his dramatic 'Good God' to arouse the Commons and the strong final sentence 'the direct reverse' and 'notorious' could be very effective in arousing total opposition to the idea that it would be wise for either the Lords or the Commons not to resist the Reform Bill.

(e) Each of the three authors/speakers were alive at the time of the Reform Bill and were informed about what was happening to it or involved in its passage in one way or another. The author of extract I seems to know what people think and has clear opinions about what is happening; his comments are dated and this is clearly primary evidence. The author of extract II is a woman and so cannot be as directly involved in politics but she too is writing immediately at the time and seems well informed. It would be interesting to the historian to know if either of these memoirs was heavily edited before being published for they would then not be so valuable. The speech to the Commons in extract III is very valuable because it gives an idea of what happened in one of the debates on reform and the flavour of some of the arguments involved. The historian should value them all highly but should not assume that all their claims are true because the extracts are the opinions of people who clearly have strong views on the issue.

(f) There is much of value in these extracts. They give ideas on the state of public opinion in 1831 and they point out both the strength of the government and the mistakes of the Opposition (extract I) and in extract II question strongly the role of Peel. All three extracts will have to be treated cautiously on matters of opinion. Extract II in particular is prejudiced against Peel and treats him as a scapegoat for the lack of effective Tory opposition to reform. The king, William IV, also gets unfairly blamed. He was never so strong a supporter of reform as extract II claims. The importance of public opinion in getting the Act passed is very clearly shown in these extracts and, in extract I, the organization of the supporters of reform is also clear.

The extracts cannot tell the whole story of the passing of the Bill. They are all dated 1831 and the Act was not passed until June 1832. The first and second extracts, March 1831, relate to the First Reform Bill which was wrecked in the Commons committee but Croker's speech (extract III) is about the second Bill introduced by the government and later defeated by the House of Lords. In fact it needed a third Bill in 1832 before parliamentary reform was passed and of course none of this appears in these extracts. To this extent the account, while revealing about both support and opposition to the idea of reform, is very incomplete.

Examiner's comments This answer was deliberately selected because it gave strong direct answers to each of the sub-questions in order to give some clues as to how an effective answer would read. It is not long but the organization is very competent and the style very mature. This is an A grade answer with very few marks dropped in any of the sub-questions. Try to learn from it how to answer extract questions but do not get depressed if this seems much more sophisticated than your own answers. Do however try to see how the candidate has related the extracts to the sub-questions and also the length of the answers to the marks available.

Extract question 2 – The rise of the Nazis to power

(a) (i)   The 1919 peace treaty imposed on Germany
    (ii) The blackshirts, a Nazi private army

(b) The main reasons given in extract I are that many young Germans supported Hitler because they wanted a very different society based on very different economic organization. They wanted the new society to be clearly German and based on 'national honour' and for this reason probably did not approve of the communists. They did not think that the 'essentially conservative' democratic parties of Weimar politicians were likely to deliver this radically new society. The young were also interested in their own futures and Hitler's promise of jobs and recovery.

(c) In extract I the possibility of the social revolution rests entirely on Hitler's promises; you either believe he can deliver or not. The main doubt about achieving the 'social revolution' comes in extract II with the comment on the party leadership having contradictory and confused views on economic policy. This suggests that not everyone among the Nazi leaders was as enthusiastic as Hitler was made to appear in extract I and so he may not be able to live up to his promises. Even more serious is the other evidence in extract II that Hitler, far from being in favour of a social revolution based on 'German socialism' was an enemy of a planned state economy and was anxious to give the great industrialists a free hand to continue to develop capitalism in order to gain the highest possible production. He does not have any idea of social revolution or 'thorough change in economic conditions' (extract I) in mind. His 'promises' look to be empty ones.

(d) Extract III very effectively shows the appeal of the Nazi Party. The content describes a mass rally, well organized to impress people with the power and energy of the Nazis. It mentions both the use of loudspeakers and the radio to reach the maximum size audience. The language adds to this impression of power and organization. Words like 'huge posters', 'slogans screamed', 'brawny arms' and 'elbowed their way' showed Nazi power in the streets. In the stadium the great number there is stressed and the 'millions' listening to the radio. Here words like 'flaunting swastikas', 'thrilling background', 'huge SA bands' and 'terrifying power' all emphasize the strength of Nazism. The tone in this extract is one of great admiration for the Nazis.

(e) A historian would be cautious because extract I is from a foreign paper and we need to know what its sources of information were. Extract II is from many years later and Funk will be anxious to clear his own name so can anything he says be trusted? Extract III was written while Hitler was at the height of his power and this may have affected what the author would risk writing publicly.

(f) In some ways these documents give a very good account of the rise of the Nazis to power. The first extract illustrates how the political message of the Nazis appealed to different groups in German society with the message of bringing better economic times to Germany and also restoring German honour. The sentence on restoring a strong Reich after the humiliation of Versailles shows a lot about the appeal of the Nazis to national pride. The third extract is a very full account of how the Nazis mobilized popular support by clever propaganda and an impression of enormous power. Propaganda played a large part in getting millions of Germans behind Hitler and the use of the radio was important to them. All this is included in the extracts and shows how Hitler built up a large public support.

But this was not all of the story of how the Nazis came to power. Even with all their support they fell short of a majority in the parliament and Hitler then had to intrigue and do deals with other right-wing politicians like Hugenberg and Von Papen. These men helped to put pressure on President Hindenburg to appoint Hitler as Chancellor. None of this important part of how the Nazis came to power is contained in the extracts. The nearest thing is in extract II where Hitler's intrigues to win the support and the money of the industrialists is clearly shown, but even here his intrigues to win the support of the German army are not mentioned. The other part of the story which is not mentioned is the violence against other politicians which the SA and the SS employed and which increased greatly once Hitler became Chancellor. So the account in the extracts is interesting but far from complete.

Examiner's comments These are strong answers to all the sub-questions. Most interesting is the answer to (f) because the candidate tries to answer the question so directly and goes on doing that. You could learn a lot from this answer about how to answer such questions which involve assessing documents against own knowledge.

Section B

British history

1 First very briefly define the criteria by which, in 1815–27, one would judge the effectiveness of any government. Keeping law and order, satisfying supporters, giving political stability, keeping taxes down, but reform was not a high priority for the political class. Then judge the Liverpool government's actions (or the most important of them) against these criteria. Remember to comment on 1822–27 as well as 1815–22.

2 Two part question: do not spend too long on the first part. The Tamworth Manifesto and the 1841 election victory are central to the first part but it is worth challenging the question to argue that it was not a new party but the old landed Tory Party which won in 1841, which was why trouble came in 1846. Peel's haste to repeal the Corn Laws did damage the party for it defied the landed interest which still dominated the party. It is worth arguing that others, especially Disraeli, who could not see the pressing national interest but who played for personal advantage, must also be blamed.

3 Start by defining 'Britain's national interests' but do it briefly – order and a balance of power in continental Europe to check over-powerful nations, encourage friendly nations in Europe, promote British trade everywhere? Then take specific instances and comment on how each helped or failed to help any of these, make a list now of the issues Palmerston was involved in and think about this. Note that most questions specify his role either between 1830 and 1841 or from 1846 to his death in 1865 so you will then need to have enough knowledge of each period to provide a full answer.

4 List the principles in the introduction then explain how the 'work' of the ministry related to the principles. Do not fall into the trap of describing all the work of the ministry and forget that the question is about principles. Draw up your own list of principles now but they should include – low taxation, free trade, minimum government expenditure so no expensive social reforms, people to stand on their own feet (self-help), equality of opportunity, Christian moral basis for policy. The question as worded includes foreign policy, so do have one paragraph on that.

5 This is the basis for standard comparative questions on Disraeli so you need to prepare all aspects of his 1874–80 ministry. Try to question whether he was responsible for all the social reform or all the imperial advances which happened. His role as international statesman at Berlin is more obviously his personal contribution and could be stressed in the answer. Be ready for other questions which invite comparison with Gladstone, 1868–74, or go back into Disraeli's earlier career from the 1840s to 1874.

6 Make the point that Labour was a working-class party and this was more important to its rise to 1914 than was socialism. Explain why other parties were not meeting working-class interest but deal especially with the Liberals who might have been expected to do so. Growth of mass trade unions and a wider electorate and new emphasis on social problems are part of the story but the deals with the Liberals which helped get more MPs are also important. In revision for an outline paper consider taking the topic through to 1929 or 1931.

7 Avoid telling the story of British foreign policy since 1900, instead put up reasons. British commitments (which need to be explained) to France and to Russia were part of the story and yet in 1914 even the cabinet hesitated. The German attack on Belgium, and why this brought Britain in, is the other issue. It needs to be widened to argue that Britain could hardly have stood by to see the continent dominated by Germany, which was in any case increasingly seen as a dangerous power (give reasons why).

8 It is easiest to dismiss the argument that the Liberal Party was, already in 1914, in a state of crisis but do so briefly. The essay can then explain how the war divided the party and made much of it a junior partner of the Conservatives. Include the reasons why the Labour Party seemed more relevant to many of the increased electorate after 1918 and how fear of socialism drove other Liberals to the security of the Conservatives. Personal rivalry between Lloyd George and Asquith prevented a post-war recovery and, once Labour became the government in 1924, the Liberals were doomed to be the third party; explain how this operated in the 1929 election but do so very briefly.

9 A very similar essay, on this common examination topic, is outlined in the topic outline on British foreign policy after 1914. The argument, from the Churchill charges to the more recent defence of Chamberlain, is well worth mastering. The theme has to be the lack of alternatives in view of the many problems facing Britain but it might be wise to acknowledge that in 1939 war did come and so the policy did fail, so that Churchill could indeed claim that he had been proved right.

10 The loss of empire has to be agreed and perhaps should be briefly explained in the introduction to the essay. The more interesting issue concerns Britain's international role and at least three strands need to be referred to:
  ▶ the continued nostalgia for an imperial role – the Suez adventure of 1956 is the best example
  ▶ the desire to see a continuation of the 'special relationship' with the USA based on common historical heritage and on partnership in the Second World War
  ▶ a reluctance to move closer to Europe which needs illustrating; the attitudes of Labour Foreign Secretary Bevin could be useful here.
The easiest route to an answer may well be to agree with the quotation.

European history

11 One line of argument could be that the Settlement arrangements were a compromise between principles and great power interests and then illustrate this from the terms. Principles include the balance of power in Europe, restoring legitimate rulers, ensuring arrangements to preserve the peace: work out which of the terms can illustrate which principles. Then look at how each of the great powers benefited and give the most telling examples of this. You could question whether principles and national interests were always opposites.

12 You need a clear final conclusion on 'to what extent' and the easiest route is to decide at the start of your essay what that is going to be. Arguably Charles X was to a large extent responsible but he also had a difficult inheritance which helped to bring about the events of 1830. You then need to give substance to both parts of this answer. The aftermath of the French Revolution had created many potential opponents for the restored Bourbons (this being the difficult 'inheritance') and with Charles's many mistakes is easily illustrated to provide a balanced answer.

13 This is another two part question: do not start it unless you feel you can deal with both parts. It would be better to have general reasons (liberalism and nationalism?), rather than a geographic survey of Europe, in order to explain why there were revolutions. The failure can also be answered by a general statement on the power of the reactionary forces and the weaknesses of the revolutionaries. General points in both parts will need to be backed by specific examples and here your knowledge of specific countries will be very useful but will need to be handled economically.

14 As with question 13, a clear view of the balance you wish to strike, firmly stated at the start of your essay, could give the answer its best structure. You could then argue (instead of describing the process of unification, for this is a topic in which long descriptive answers with much irrelevance are notorious) that at key points foreign intervention was crucial but that this is only part of the explanation of unification. You could follow this by a few lines on what the contributions of Mazzini, Cavour and Garibaldi, all Italians, were and how important each was to unification. Note the student answer to a similar question on pp. 86–7.

15 Again, as with the two previous questions, a clear view should be offered at the beginning of the essay, so setting up the structure of your argument. Variations on this topic are so common that you should work out the balance to strike as part of your revision activity but do not go into the examination with a prepared script or you might well be thrown into confusion by an unusually worded question. Bismarck was clearly very important to unification and how needs to be explained, but other factors, William II, the mistakes of Austria-Hungary and of Napoleon III, the strength of German nationalism, the fears of the south German states at French 'aggression' and even the role of chance could be referred to in order to suggest that the essay title is over-simple.

16 Yet another two part question so give attention to both parts. The decline of the Ottoman Empire, the rising national ambitions of the Christian inhabitants of the European part of the Empire, the role of Austria-Hungary and the ambitions of Russia are at the heart of any explanation of the tension. The easiest way to answer the second part may well be to argue that the Congress led to a short-term easing of tension (illustrate how) but solved none of the issues in the long term (also elaborate this).

17 A straightforward start would be to explain that one 'camp' already existed in 1890 and indicate what that was. Do not however be drawn back to a blow by blow account of Bismarck's foreign policy. You can then explain how the Franco-Russian-British 'camp' emerged in response via various crises. Note that you also have to explain 'armed' so you will need some discussion of the arms race. Be aware that the end date is 1907, so do not waste time taking the story through to 1914.

18 Here you have to explain first why Mussolini became Prime Minister in 1922 and then why he and the fascists were able to build up absolute power in the state by 1929. Such a task may feature in outline papers but this is also a popular option paper topic and, in such papers, the focus may well be either on 1922 or on the later build-up of power. You will then need to have enough ideas and information to deal with such more tightly focused questions. In the second part of this question both the appeal of the fascists to many Italian people and also the weaknesses of possible opponents of the fascists should be covered. Have some specific examples ready.

19 One answer would be to agree that some people achieved things that they wanted under the Nazis, improved employment prospects, roads and public works, restored national prestige at home and abroad. You could then question whether the economic gains were all that great and point to the massive bureaucracy and the over-manning of inefficient industries. Many 'gains' were only propaganda. The bulk of the essay may well be on the 'price paid' and here you need to be fully informed and not only in terms of the persecution of the Jews. A few examples of pressure to conform with state holidays, membership of the Hitler Youth, businessmen having to contribute to party funds, the abolition of political parties and independent trade unions – prepare such a list of examples of life under the Nazis as part of your examination revision.

20 Both parts of the question must have attention. Argue that the purge of the kulaks in the early 1930s had a serious economic purpose but that the later political purges did not and were a result of Stalin's paranoia. The danger of the early purges depends on your view of the collectivisation of agriculture, which was arguably a great step forward in socialist planning and economic development. The later purges did bring great harm to industry with the loss of many managers, to the defence of the country with the loss of many of the officer class and to millions of individuals. All this will need illustrating.